PENGUIN BOOKS

THE LIFE IT BRINGS

Since receiving his Ph.D. from Harvard University in 1955, Jeremy Bernstein has lectured and taught at universities here and abroad on the theory of elementary particles and cosmology.

In 1961 he joined *The New Yorker* as a staff writer, a position he still holds. He is the author of numerous physics papers and of twelve books, among them the classic study of the computer, *The Analytical Engine*, and the story of Bell Labs, *Three Degrees Above Zero*. He also writes a biennial column for *The American Scholar*, "Out of My Mind." The awards he has received for his writing include a Westinghouse-AAAS Science Writing Prize, a Brandeis Creative Arts Medal, and a National Book Award nomination for his biography *Einstein*.

Mr. Bernstein is a professor at the Stevens Institute of Technology in Hoboken, New Jersey, and an adjunct professor at the Rockefeller University. He lives in New York City.

THE
LIFE
IT
BRINGS

Penguin Books

One
Physicist's
Beginnings

Jeremy
Bernstein

PENGUIN BOOKS
Published by the Penguin Group
Viking Penguin Inc., 40 West 23rd Street, New York, New York 10010, U.S.A.
Penguin Books Ltd, 27 Wrights Lane, London W8 5TZ, England
Penguin Books Australia Ltd, Ringwood, Victoria, Australia
Penguin Books Canada Ltd, 2801 John Street, Markham, Ontario, Canada L3R 1B4
Penguin Books (N.Z.) Ltd, 182–190 Wairau Road, Auckland 10, New Zealand

Penguin Books Ltd, Registered Offices:
Harmondsworth, Middlesex, England

First published in the United States of America by
Ticknor & Fields 1987.
Published in Penguin Books 1988

Most of this book originally appeared, in slightly different form, in *The New Yorker*.

The author is grateful to Peter Oppenheimer for permission to reprint selections from letters
written by his father, J. Robert Oppenheimer, and to the Hebrew University of Jerusalem,
Israel, for permission to reprint a letter from Albert Einstein to the author.
Thanks are also gratefully extended to the following for their courtesy in permitting the
use of photographs:
The American Institute of Physics Niels Bohr Library for the photo by Alan W. Richards
of T. D. Lee and C. N. Yang.
The Cruft Laboratory Photographic Department, Harvard University, for the photos of I.
Bernard Cohen and Wendell Furry by Paul Donaldson, and for the photo of Julian Schwinger.
We also thank Julian Schwinger for permission to use the photograph of him.
The Institute for Advanced Study in Princeton, New Jersey, for the photos of the Institute
and of Freeman Dyson.
The MIT Museum for the photos of Philipp Frank and Murray Gell-Mann, and for the
photograph by Calvin Campbell of Francis Low and Kenneth Johnson.
Peter Oppenheimer for the photo of J. Robert Oppenheimer.

LIBRARY OF CONGRESS CATALOGING IN PUBLICATION DATA
Bernstein, Jeremy, 1929–
The life it brings.
Reprint. Originally published: New York: Ticknor &
Fields, 1987.
1. Bernstein, Jeremy, 1929– . 2. Physicists—
United States—Biography. I. Title.
[QC16.B458A3 1988] 530′.092′4 [B] 87-32821
ISBN 0 14 01.0988 9

Printed in the United States of America by
R. R. Donnelley & Sons Company, Harrisonburg, Virginia
Set in Trump Mediaeval

To My Parents

Acknowledgments

In preparing this book and the associated *New Yorker* articles I have had the help of Katrina Kenison and Frances Apt of Ticknor & Fields and William Shawn and Sara Lippincott of *The New Yorker*. I am grateful both to them and to Jocelyn Carlson for their help and encouragement.

Contents

Preface

As I write these words, two photographs look down on me, photographs of two of the men I admire most — Albert Einstein and J. Robert Oppenheimer. The photographs are in their own way deeply revealing. Einstein has his tongue out, like a child. I believe that the occasion of this photograph was Einstein's seventy-second birthday. He had been asked to smile by the photographers, whom he referred to as *licht Affen* (light apes). So he stuck out his tongue at them in an amiable way: Einstein sticking out his tongue at the establishment yet once again. Oppenheimer's photograph is equally characteristic. He is wearing one of his tailor-made three-piece suits; in his left hand there is a lighted cigarette. His expression is that odd mixture of wariness and a touch of feline cruelty which Oppenheimer often wore during the years I knew him, after his trial. Part of his neck is visible, and it is the weather-worn neck of someone who has spent a good deal of time in the sun. Looking at his face, you would be hard put to guess his profession, but it is clearly the face of *someone.* The curious thing about this particular photograph is that if I turn it sideways to the light, I can see that it is autographed and dedicated to my father. No date is given, but the dedication reads, "To Rabbi Bernstein; with respect, Robert Oppenheimer." I have no idea of how or when my father got this photograph. I feel quite sure that it had nothing to do with me, as I am sure that at the time Oppenheimer signed the photograph I had not yet met him. That would happen later.

My father, Oppenheimer, Einstein, and I are four points through which I can trace all sorts of lines. The course my life has taken has drawn these lines for me; what I want to do is try to re-create this course. I will begin at the beginning but I will not end at the end; that is, I will not describe my life after I became a university professor and a professional writer. As a writer, I once invented an entire comic university, and now I have gotten tenure there — in the sense that real universities and the one of my imagination have become hopelessly entwined. So I will explain instead how, after an unlikely beginning, I became a physicist. Unlike Frank Oppenheimer, I had no older brother to write me a letter like the one Robert sent Frank in 1926, when Frank was thirteen:

> And still more advice: I don't think you would enjoy reading about relativity very much until you have studied a little geometry, a little mechanics, a little electro-dynamics. But if you want to try, Eddington's book is the best to start on. I remember that five years ago you were dressed up to act like Albert Einstein; in a few years it seems, they won't need to disguise you. And you'll be able to write your own speech. And now a final word of advice: try to understand really, to your own satisfaction, thoroughly and honestly, the few things in which you are most interested: because it is only when you have learnt to do that, when you realize how hard and how very satisfying it is, that you will appreciate fully the

more spectacular things like relativity and mechanistic biology. If you think I am wrong please don't hesitate to tell me so. I'm only talking from my own very small experience.

Nor did I have a Robert Oppenheimer to write to me as he did to Frank eight years later: "I take it that Cambridge has been right for you, and that physics has gotten now very much under your skin, physics and the obvious excellences of the life it brings." What a wonderful phrase — "the obvious excellences of the life it brings." That is what this book is about: a life in physics and the obvious excellences it has brought.

1

Tuesday's Child

I HAVE ALWAYS MARVELED at writers who seem to have total recall of their childhood, even their very early years. I have little coherent recollection of my own. I think I could make up a childhood by looking at the pictures in my "baby book" and the photograph album my mother recently put together for her three children. But the little boy staring out of these pictures — sometimes wearing a sailor suit and sometimes not — could be anyone. In many of the pictures this child is someone I don't even think I would have liked very much; too often he looks wary and fearful, or is smiling for no apparent reason, perhaps to please the photographer. I much prefer the pictures of my brother and sister.

I was born on December 31, 1929, a Tuesday, in Rochester, New York. My father, Philip, who was born in Rochester in 1901, had returned to the city in late 1926 to become the assistant rabbi and then the rabbi of a large and old Reform congregation, Temple B'rith Kodesh, founded in 1848. His parents had emigrated as very young people from Lithuania. I have never been able to get an intelligible account of why my grandmother's family, the Steinbergs, settled in Rochester. It has always seemed such an archetypal middle-class, middle-American city that I cannot imagine what would have possessed Jews from a *shtetl* in Lithuania to choose it over, say, Cleveland or St. Louis.

My father's father did not immediately settle in Rochester, or, I gather, anywhere else. Having arrived in this country at fourteen or fifteen, he became an itinerant peddler of one thing and another, and he found my grandmother on one of his upstate New York tours and remained there. He later became a tailor and, when I first knew him, had a small, unbelievably dusty shop near the railroad station. In his later years he spent a lot of time in the station itself, where he had made friends among the railroad personnel. He sold pants that he said "wore like iron," and what he called "remlets" — bits of cloth left over from the pants. One of the horrors of my childhood was having to wear my grandfather's pants, which both wore and felt like iron. Neither my grandmother nor my grandfather had much, if any, formal education. Nonetheless, my grandmother, who was eleven or twelve when she left Lithuania, had taught herself to read while still in the shtetl in the village of Serage — a remarkable achievement for a young girl, given the shtetl mores — and she read letters, and wrote them, for her illiterate fellow shtetl dwellers. Other than that, I am unaware of much intellectual distinction in the ancestry on this side of the family. In later years my father, who was an extraordinarily handsome man, and my uncle Milton Steinberg, also extremely attractive and the rabbi of a large Conservative congregation in New York City, had a picture taken of the two of them holding each other's noses. It is a playful picture and one of them had written on it that the other was descended from a long line of "horse thieves and peddlers," something that, as far as I know, may well have applied to both of them, although Milton Steinberg's father was a great Talmudic scholar.

On my mother's side, the Rubins, we are of Russian descent. My mother, Sophie, recently informed me that her parents came from the outskirts of Minsk and Pinsk, but she is not sure who came from which. (Her younger sister, Alice, for whom my sister was eventually named, told me that she had a mnemonic for sorting this out which went, "Mom is from Minsk. Pop is from Pinsk.") She also told me that she had never asked her mother how she met her father. Our family has always had little interest in its history. But there is no question as to why my Russian grandfather came here: he was escaping from the czar's recruiting officers. One of his favorite expressions was "Who can tell it, a thing like this?" which I think summarized his feelings about the czar's army. He told me more than once about being hidden in a horse-drawn cart and driven to the border — which border I can no longer remember. And he ended up in Brooklyn, where my mother was born.

I was always impressed by what he did for a living: he manufactured metal plumbing fixtures in a small factory located under the Brooklyn Bridge. It was called Superior Brass and sometimes manufactured plumbing parts for ocean liners while they were in port. I liked to go there and watch the fixtures being created out of the raw metal like sculptures, trailing great spiral festoons of shiny metal as they were being machined. His work appealed to me because it was neither spiritual nor cerebral. By the time I was old enough to appreciate what different people's work was like, I had discovered that I had four close relatives who were university professors and three who were rabbis. It was a relief to have one or two who actually made something tangible.

My father was educated in the Rochester public schools — P.S. 10 and P.S. 14 and then East High School, where, I have been told, he was an exceptional student. When it came time for him to go to college, he chose Syracuse University rather than the University of Rochester or Cornell, where his two younger brothers later went. He thought he might go into the law — he had been a brilliant high school debater — and in fact was later accepted at Harvard Law School. Though there was precious little money in the Bernstein household, my father did manage to borrow forty dollars toward tuition. He joined Sigma Alpha Mu, one of the Jewish fraternities at Syracuse, and did various jobs around the fraternity. He sold fruit — later in life his fraternity brothers would kid him by saying that it had been of dubious quality — and my grandfather's pants, which were *certainly* of dubious quality. To pay for his meals he waited on table.

During this time my father taught Sunday school, at a dollar a Sunday, for Rabbi Benjamin Friedman of Syracuse. He acquired both a taste for the life of a rabbi and the love of my mother, Rabbi Friedman's niece, who was a student of art and design at the Pratt Institute in New York City. Recently she told me that she had won a scholarship to study design in Paris and would have gone had she not fallen in love with my father.

I don't know what my father's major was in college; possibly philosophy. He never mentioned any professor, as I recall, who made a special impression on him. His most influential teacher was Stephen Wise, of the Jewish Institute of Religion, where he went in 1922, as a member of the institute's first class, to study for the rabbinate. My brother, Stephen, is named after Rabbi Wise. After my sister, Alice, was born either Wise or my father said, "*Das ist alles,*" a pun that the family kept alive. My father was a highly educated and cultivated man, but in specific areas. He was quite unmusical; he never discussed music with us, and I don't remember his discussing literature either, although there was a time when he read P. G. Wodehouse aloud to us. In science and mathematics he was a near cipher. I think the subjects made him uncomfortable, more so after I got into them. When I was at Harvard, taking mathematics courses during most summers as well as the winters, he came to Cambridge for a visit. A celebrated Eastern European mathematician was teaching my summer course, and my father sat in. At one point the professor leaned toward my father, whose provenance must have been something of a mystery, and said, in a thick accent, "Mathematics is not like *New York Times*. We do not give all news that is fit to print." My father's only response to this odd piece of intelligence was to pass me a note containing a formula of his own devising: "IF2P."

After his final year at the Jewish Institute of Religion, when he was twenty-three, my father won a fellowship, which permitted him to study abroad for a year. He planned to marry my mother on his return. His notion, as he explained it to her, was that she would not go out with anyone else while he was away. My mother, who was eighteen, told him that, though she loved him very much, she had every intention of going out while he was away. He promptly married her and they went abroad together. It must have been an extraordinary trip — those two very handsome young people on a journey of high adventure. They went to the Soviet Union out of curiosity and then, in 1926, my father enrolled in the first class ever convened in the Hebrew University in Jerusalem. That was preceded by a time in Cambridge, England, from which came his thesis and, three years later, my name.

His thesis was on Jeremiah, and when I was born that is what he wanted to call me. My mother, however, thought Jeremiah "a very long name for a small boy," so I became Jeremy, a name that caused me much embarrassment when I was a child. Neither my schoolmates nor my teachers seemed able to get it right. Sometimes I was Johnny and sometimes Germy and finally Jerry, of which my parents disapproved. Nevertheless, I stayed Jerry until I began to write professionally. Then I signed my articles with my real name and became Jeremy once and for all.

The strange little boy who looks at me — when he does look at me and not down or to the side — from my baby book is a pretty child with large dark eyes. My first recollection of that child as myself is of being photographed in my father's lap. The year was probably 1934, and my father had just come back from a trip to Germany, where he had gone to see the Nazi phenomenon at first hand. He brought me a sailor suit and a sailor doll, and I recall — or think I do — the feel of the stones on the porch as I sat, waiting for him to put me on his lap. I was wearing the suit and holding the doll while the picture was taken. The photograph was published in the newspaper — my father had quickly become a prominent citizen of Rochester — and I still have it. I have absolutely no early scientific or mathematical memories — none. That is why I am so interested in those of my friends and colleagues. Freeman Dyson, for example, told me that when he was still young enough "to have been put down for naps," he invented for himself the idea of the convergent infinite series. He began adding up the fractions $1/2 + 1/4 + 1/8 + 1/16 + \ldots$ and observed that the sum approached closer and closer to 1. And Dyson's teacher

Hans Bethe told me that when he was four or five, he already understood fractions and decimals and that he kept a notebook which he filled with such things as the powers of 10. My only memories of this kind have to do with playing a game in which my father gave me, orally, a list of small numbers to add and subtract in my head. Sometimes he did this when there were guests for dinner, and I would go under the dining room table, where I could concentrate better. I remember the groves of feet and shoes that I crawled among until I found an isolated place to do the calculations. I also remember being given a "special problem" to solve when I was in the sixth or seventh grade. It consisted of finding the circumference of a racetrack with two straight sides closed by two semi-circular ends, so I must have known the formula for the circumference of a circle.

Across the street from our house there lived an older boy whose real name now eludes me. We called him Bud. My own nickname during those early years was Snookie. Bud and Snookie. Bud was a sort of technological polymath. He built and raced soap-box cars — cars on which you could ride — made of wooden crates, little wheels, and assorted parts scrounged from here and there. He also built shortwave radios and sent and received messages over them. I admired all of this activity immensely and tried to imitate it. I didn't build cars but I did make radios. This may sound impressive, but the truth is that I didn't understand what I was doing and lacked the intellectual discipline to find out. It was no harder to build a radio than to build a model airplane, which I also did. I just followed the directions in a kit or circuit diagram. There were things known as resistors, but I didn't have the foggiest idea what they were for. Their electrical properties were measured in units called ohms, and they were color-coded for different magnitudes. That was all I knew about them. When I needed resistors to build a radio, I would go to a radio parts store and order them. It all sounded very grand, but I never took the next step of asking what they were for or how a radio actually worked. Bud disappeared into the adolescent world of high school, and there was no one else around who had any interest in making radios. I let the whole matter drop.

The neighborhood we lived in had, I think, only four Jewish families. Whether it had been my father's intention or not, his choice of neighborhood isolated our family to some extent from his congregation. Perhaps there are children of clergymen who like their role. I didn't. I was a private child and found it deeply embarrassing to be scrutinized or patted by members of my father's congregation, most of whom I did not know. The last time I felt this discomfort was at my father's funeral. My mother, brother, sister, and I were led from a small private room into the great hall of the synagogue, in full view of the vast congregation, to confront, for the first time, my father in his coffin. I felt that our private grief had become a spectacle for others; the feeling brought back all those memories of being the rabbi's son.

In my case, being the rabbi's son meant setting certain kinds of examples. My father explained many times that I had to go to Hebrew school to set an example. I had to go to services on Friday night to set an example. I had to have a large and elaborate Bar Mitzvah to set an example . . . and so on, and so on. In my own private — and sometimes not so private — ways, I rebelled. I had one fantasy in which, at the climax of the Friday night service, when my father would dramatically open the Ark of the Covenant to remove the Torah, a great, hairy arm would come out and sweep him inside, closing the curtains behind. I shared this scenario with my best friend of the time, Richard Epstein, now a distinguished microbiologist, who was also sent to temple on Friday nights to set an example. We got ourselves into a state of uncontrollable giggles, made the worse for our trying to suppress them. The example we set was not exactly what everyone had in mind, and we were not allowed to sit next to each other on subsequent Friday nights.

I had ambivalent feelings about my father's work. I knew — I was told often enough — that he was a very distinguished man. Max Hertzberger, one of the members of his congregation and the first physicist I ever met, wrote to his family in Germany, "In Rochester we have a rabbi of such distinction that he is invited to preach not only in Christian churches but also in other Jewish synagogues." During the time that my father was president of the Rochester City Club, people like Clarence Darrow would stay at our house. (Darrow, incidentally, gave my father a Bible he inscribed "With Compliments of the Author.") On the other hand, my father's work was unlike the work done by the fathers of the boys I admired in my neighborhood. Eddie Lays's father, for instance, was a machinist at the Gleason Works; Jack Poray's father owned a gas station. Both Eddie and Jack were first-rate athletes — Jack was the first person I ever saw who could hit a baseball from either side of the plate — and what they did and what their fathers did seemed to me to be real, concrete. What my father did seemed almost alien. The whole matter was symbolized in my mind by the matter of sleds. Rochester was and is known for its almost interminable snowy winters. I enjoyed those winters and engaged in all the appropriate sports. But one had to have a sled. Because a member of my father's congregation sold sleds, we could get them wholesale. The problem was that they were the *wrong* sleds. Eddie Lays, Jack Poray, and nearly everyone else had a Flexible Flyer; I had a strange sled, in some way not quite correct. No doubt it was perfectly good if the question was simply sledding, but Flexible Flyers came, in my mind, to represent that other world, to which I felt I did not belong. Later, when I started to go out with girls, long-legged, Scandinavian-looking blondes became Flexible Flyers.

Since my father was a Reform rabbi, I never had the kind of cultural confrontation with him that other scientists I know have had with their families on breaking out of the confines of Orthodox Jewry. I. I. Rabi, for example, told me that it was his discovery, in 1908, of the Copernican system in a little book in the Brooklyn public library that led him to question his parents' belief that, as he put it, "the earth is flat and that there is a big fish, the Leviathan, which surrounds it, which has its own tail in its mouth, and which will be eaten on the Day of Judgment by the good Orthodox Jews while the others will get nothing." I don't recall ever being asked what I *believed*, which was just as well, since I didn't believe in any theological doctrine, Jewish or otherwise. To my parents, the important thing was that I behave in certain ways, acknowledging certain symbols.

My father's mother was Orthodox. She kept a kosher home and lived in an Orthodox Jewish neighborhood in Rochester. I never asked my father how she felt about his becoming a Reform rabbi. She did attend his temple, especially on Saturday mornings, when the more traditional services were held. We went to her house on some of the Jewish holidays, like Passover. The meals she served, with foods like matzoh ball soup and *tsimmes*, always made me uncomfortable: What would Eddie Lays and Jack Poray think? I couldn't wait to get back to what I thought of as *my* neighborhood. All of this prevented me from getting to know my grandmother well until shortly before her death. I spent some time with her alone then and realized that underneath what had seemed an impenetrable layer of grandmotherly platitudes was a woman with a keen mind and an unsentimental view of the strengths and weaknesses of her family.

Among the things one doesn't know or tends to forget — if one is a comfortably integrated American Jew in the 1980s — was how overt anti-Semitism was in the 1930s, when I was growing up. There was, of course, the rabid public anti-Semitism of a man like Father Coughlin, whose radio sermons we used to listen to at home with morbid attention. But what was encountered more often was the anti-Semitism of those whom my father called the "gentle people of prejudice." There were playmates you thought of as friends who, in a moment of pique, would call you a dirty Jew. There were places — country clubs, for example — where Jews were not meant to go, and other places where it was not clear whether Jews were meant to go. I have a vivid recollection of setting off in our Essex car with my parents and my brother to spend a summer weekend in a hotel in the Finger Lakes, not far from home. It was to have been a festive occasion. When we arrived at the hotel, where my father had made reservations, he left us in the car and went inside to make sure everything was in order. He came out ashen-faced. It was always my father's policy to confront anti-Semitism head on, and he made a point of not patronizing hotels that did not accept Jews, even if we could have gotten in by inadvertence. So he had told the manager that he was *Rabbi* Bernstein. The manager said that we were not welcome, and we returned, miserable, to Rochester.

This was, of course, only a minor inconvenience; my father was aware of what was happening in Germany. He had been there as late as 1938, when the four of us — Alice was not born until the following year — took a trip to Europe and the Middle East. My mother, Stephen, and I remained in England while my father went to Germany, where he saw for himself what was taking place in that wretched country. After our return, he had a hand in bringing German refugees to Rochester and in making them feel welcome there. Considering the multitudes who were soon to be murdered, those who escaped were a pathetic trickle, but among them were some extraordinary people, including Max Hertzberger. I am convinced that Hertzberger, who died a few years ago, was a genius. Trained as a physicist in Berlin, taught by Einstein — who had examined him on his Ph.D. thesis — Hertzberger was one of the foremost designers of optical lenses and had been employed by Zeiss before he and his family were thrown out of Germany. He had written the book on geometrical optics in the famous Yellow Peril series — so called for the yellow covers — put out by Springer Verlag in Germany. He was also a very eccentric man. I remember once being with him while he made a phone call in German. After finishing the call, he did not realize that he was still speaking German; I could not get him to switch back into English and finally gave up. He was a very strong chess player and later, when I was in high school and college, gave me some chess lessons. At Eastman Kodak, where he worked when he came to this country, he made, I believe, some important innovations in lens design.

My relationship with Hertzberger had three distinct phases. Before the war, when I was still a child, I remember him only because he talked about Albert Einstein. In our family Einstein was an exemplar of everything that was best, although my father made no pretense of understanding his physics. I doubt he even had any interest. In later years he would ask me about it, and when I would start to explain, he'd change the subject. Hertzberger, however, was ready to discuss the theory of relativity at the drop of a hat, and once he started, he was relentless. I remember, with a feeling of affection for poor Max, the story my father told us about a garden party, given shortly before the war, to welcome the newly arrived refugees. The hostess had heard that Max had had an association with Einstein and was curious to hear a bit about relativity. Max took off on an extended discourse about space, time, Riemannian geometry, and heaven knows what while, unbeknownst to him, an elegant small dog was delicately irrigating his shoe. I heard this story at an age where it struck me as the ne plus ultra of high humor.

The second phase of my relationship with Max was the happiest. By the time I'd finished my college freshman year, I was determined to learn the theory of relativity myself. Back home in Rochester, I sought out Max for his help. In retrospect I can see how naïve this was. I did not have sufficient grounding even to understand what had motivated Einstein to formulate relativity, let alone to grasp what the theory was all about. Furthermore, not until much later did I realize that Hertzberger had an idiosyncratic formulation of the theory based on a geometrical optics model. To Max it was all so self-evident that he simply could not put himself in the place of a novice; it was a total intellectual mismatch. Nonetheless, the subject fascinated me. I was equally fascinated by Max's views on the quantum theory, another topic about which I knew little. Even more of a classical physicist than Einstein, Max was troubled by the use in the quantum theory of so-called complex numbers — numbers that can be represented as points in a plane rather than points on a line. As I now think back on it, this concern is incomprehensible to me, as it must have been to Einstein. Max had sent him a paper in which he described what he called a "solution" to the complex number problem. Einstein wrote back a terse letter, in German, which Max translated for me: "Since I do not understand your problem, I do not understand your solution." But Max was so persuasive, and I was so ignorant and eager to help Max convince others of the soundness of his ideas, that some years later I helped arrange for him to give a colloquium at Harvard. I am afraid that it was not much of a success; the audience didn't understand what Max's problem was either. The sad thing for me was that, within a year or so, I no longer understood what it was myself, and this led to the third stage of our relationship. I have never been very good at simulating enthusiasm. The more I got into conventional physics, the less meaningful to me were Hertzberger's ideas on relativity theory and, above all, on the quantum theory. I tried to avoid discussing these subjects with Max, but he must have known how I felt. There was nothing I could do about it.

All of this came much later. During the time I have been describing I became convinced that I had a serious mental affliction known as "grasshopper mind." I was an

avid reader of comic books of all kinds, and in the back
of these wonderful magazines were classified ads. When
I could scrounge up enough money, I sent away for innumerable magic rings, some of which were supposed to
change color according to the wearer's shifting emotions.
One of the repeated ads showed an unfortunate man with
a cartoon balloon coming out of his head containing a
jumble of indecisive thoughts. The man was afflicted
with a terrible case of grasshopper mind. I was sure I had
it, too; I seemed to be so unfocused. It was radios one day;
skis the next; and Harriet Dorsey, the next-door girl with
whom I had rigged up a telegraph system, bedroom to
bedroom, the third. You could send away for a treatment
of grasshopper mind, but the cure was, to me, prohibi-
tively expensive. I resigned myself to suffering from it,
probably forever. There were also the *Big Little Books* —
short fat books of comics — and it was through these that
I first earned money as a writer.

When I was nine years old I was sent away to a summer camp near Rochester. I hated everything about it,
every minute I was there. I disliked the lack of privacy; I
disliked the weed-ridden lake; above all, I disliked the
"educational activities," which included cutting up an-
esthetized frogs. If *that* was science, you could have it. I
reacted to my misery by developing a low-grade fever that
put me in the infirmary. At least there was some privacy
there. My parents sent me great packages of *Big Little
Books*, which I read from morning until night. Finally,
when I showed no improvement, they took me home —
an instant cure. While still in the infirmary, however, I
had noted that there was a contest with a cash prize for
the person who could write in seventy-five words or less
just what *Big Little Books* meant to him, and when I got

home, I composed my piece. I still have the original:

> Dear sirs:
>
> I enjoy big littele books. When I was sick at camp big littele books were the only thing that kept me from going nuts. I have read many of the big littele books on your list. The reason why I like your books is because there is always somthing new and exciting. It always gives me a thrill when I get one.
>
> Sincerely yours,
Jeremy Bernstein

My skeptical but willing parents sent off this succinct document to the Whitman Publishing Company in Racine, Wisconsin, and on December 15, 1939, in a letter addressed to Master Jeremy Bernstein, came the astonishing news that I had won second place and a prize of seventy-five dollars, an enormous sum in those post-Depression years. Recently my mother reminded me that I wanted to spend the money immediately and had to be restrained. Eventually I bought a shortwave radio with part of it.

On Sunday, December 7, 1941, while my grandmother was visiting us, the news over the radio that we were at war. Grandmother began to cry; she was sure that her sons and perhaps her grandsons would have to fight. My father had had a stint of military training at the end of World War I at Fort Devens, in Massachusetts, and in Plattsburgh, where he trained for a commission. The training repelled him, especially the portion in which recruits were taught to drive bayonets into straw dummies and then twist them to enlarge the wound. He hated that. But with the rise of Hitler, he lost his pacifism. Soon after the United States entered the war, my father was asked to be the civilian head of all the Jewish chaplains in the armed forces. Within a few months we moved to New York City, and he became executive director of the Committee on Army and Navy Activities of the National Jewish Welfare Board.

I have often asked myself what course my life would have taken if my family hadn't moved. I have no idea whether I would have followed them, but in a sense my plans had already been laid. Several things were clear to me. The first was that I was not going to become a rabbi. Though I was not yet in my teens, I knew that I had no vocation. My father easily established rapport with people, and they sought him out. I already knew that my career, whatever it was to be, would require my keeping people at a certain distance. I also knew that I was not going to be a doctor; a few frog dissections had convinced me of that. One of my mother's brothers is a distinguished biochemist, and in one of my grasshopper states I had experimented with a hobby chemistry set. It was better than cutting up frogs, but I soon lost interest. I did not even know what a physicist was, notwithstanding my family's admiration for Einstein. Despite all this, I thought I could see the future shape of my life.

I would go to East High School, as my father had done. I would go to Syracuse University, too, and would join his fraternity. In fact during one of my visits with him to Syracuse I had even signed a book in his fraternity, pledging my future: "Jerry Bernstein S.A.M. 1951." Then I would study law, as he had thought of doing, and would return to Rochester to marry one of the Flexible Flyers — Harriet Dorsey, Jean Schmanke, or Virginia Baker. These were my plans, and none of them came to pass.

2

The A Train

I CAN REMEMBER hearing my mother cry only once during my entire childhood. It must have been in the late fall or early winter of 1942. My father had already gone to New York to run the Jewish chaplaincy program and had established himself in the Gramercy Park Hotel, leaving the rest of us temporarily in Rochester. I don't recall that his absence made a profound difference to me, but it must have been very hard on my mother.

Then the time came for us to move to New York and join my father in the apartment he had found for us all. My mother cried because she would be giving up her lovely home, with its lawns and little garden, for a New York apartment. I was miserable at hearing my mother cry and at the thought of leaving my school and my friends for a life I could not begin to imagine. For my parents the move was to be an interval; my father had every intention of returning to Rochester once the war was over. I suppose I thought I would go back, too, but as it turned out I never did, at least not to live.

The apartment my father had taken was on the corner of Central Park West and Eighty-fourth Street, in an area then known as the Golden Ghetto. The whole Upper West Side of New York is now so gentrified that it is hard to believe what it was like in the 1940s. There were the big apartment houses along Central Park and then, immediately to the west, brownstones — the kind that are now worth fortunes — which were said to house dangerous riffraff. I don't know who really lived in them, but in those early years in New York I always felt scared when I walked west to Broadway, where once again the houses became large and grand, and on to the Hudson River.

The dangers of New York, as perceived by our family, extended to the public schools. In Rochester it would have been unthinkable for any of us to attend a private school; apart from the cost, it would have been against my father's democratic principles. But given the family mythology about New York, my parents decided to send my brother and me to private school. The one that had been recommended was Columbia Grammar School, on West Ninety-third Street, not far from Central Park. I was enrolled there in the eighth grade in the spring semester of 1943.

I still have each of the yearbooks — the *Columbiana* — for the years 1944 through 1947, the four years I attended the school. The pictures that look out at me from these yearbooks are even stranger to me than the ones in my baby book. Almost none of the names means anything to me now. Whatever has happened, for example, to Paul S. Newlinger, of the class of 1946, who wrote in my book, "*Soy muy terrifico*"? Or Robert B. Schwaid, of the class of 1947, who wrote, "The Hell with the rest remember Robert B. Schwaid"? A few names do mean something. There is Henry Steiner, my closest friend in school, with whom I later went off to Harvard. There is Gary Graffman, known as Graflex, who was already a piano virtuoso. And there was Murray Gell-Mann. I shall have more to say about him; here it is enough to note that he would go on to dominate my field of physics — the theory of elementary particles — for well over a decade. He was awarded the Nobel Prize in Physics in 1969 for his contributions to the theory of elementary particles. He appears only in my 1944 yearbook. We are the same age, but at fourteen he was a senior. Under Senior Statistics — along with Most Popular, Howard Weinstein; and Most Likely to Succeed, Bill Goodman — there is Most Studious: "In a shower of votes, Murray Gell-Mann, the 'wonder boy' easily won the title." At fifteen he matriculated at Yale.

I don't recognize myself in these yearbook pictures. I became very fat in high school; in my sophomore year I weighed over two hundred pounds, forty pounds more than I weigh now. I don't think I gained all of that weight because I was unhappy. I gained it because I ate a lot of the wrong foods and because I came from a home and background where health and prosperity were associated with being fat. When my father was a boy, the problem for his parents had been getting enough food on the table for family survival.

I say that I was not unhappy, this requires some qualification. The adjustment to the new school was not easy. Indeed, on my first day there I was beaten up. The students were being taken for a walk around the reservoir in Central Park — what is now the jogging track — when a rat-faced kid in my class jumped me without warning. It was not a severe beating, but I was thoroughly shaken. Each of my parents reacted characteristically. My mother went to the school and made it very plain that that was not what she was paying private school tuition for. My father said that I had better learn how to take care of my-

self — to fight back. (He was beyond intimidation. In
1932, for example, when no public auditorium in Rochester would give Margaret Sanger a platform from which
to discuss her views on birth control, my father let her
speak in the auditorium of the temple, even though the
Catholic Diocese of Rochester accused her, and by impli-
cation him, of breaking the law.) I do not remember
whether I was given boxing lessons, but I do know that I
was strongly encouraged to take part in every kind of
team sport, including tackle football.

Tackle football, and then swimming, became a big
part of my high school life. In football I had an advantage
and a disadvantage. The advantage was my girth. I played
the line, and more or less by standing there could keep
opponents from breaking through. The disadvantage was
my myopia, which had been discovered several years earlier, when I ran into a tree while riding a bicycle. Because
contact lenses didn't yet exist, I played football with the
naked eye, so hostile looming shapes came and went in a
sort of haze. I stood on the line like some sort of befud-
dled, myopic sloth, grabbing at the odd human form as it
went by.

When the football season ended, the swimming season began; it lasted through March. From December to
April the whites of my eyes were an odd shade of pink as
a result of constant exposure to the chlorine in innumerable swimming pools. Our swimming team — which in
my sophomore year placed third in the National Inter-
scholastic Championships and was easily the best team
in New York City — reflected an interesting sociological
fact about the school. Nearly all the students were from
upper-middle-class Jewish families. There were a few exceptions, many of whom had been recruited to the school

on athletic scholarships, especially for swimming. When I was a sophomore, we tied the Yale freshman team — a remarkable accomplishment, since Yale was then the preeminent power in collegiate competitive swimming. My own event was the 220-yard freestyle, and I took a third in that meet — not too astonishing, for I am obliged to report that there were only three of us swimming.

Team sports were only one aspect of my new life in New York. Apart from my studies, which occupied the minimum time possible, the rest of my life was a combination of music and "show business." To explain this I have to backtrack a little. One of the best features of the Rochester public school system was its music program. In addition to being given music appreciation courses, we were each administered a test for musical aptitude. The test had to do both with pitch and rhythm, and any student who manifested aptitude was encouraged to take up a musical instrument. There was no question, in my case, of my parents' buying several instruments for me to try out, but they could rent different ones. At least in the beginning, there was a nominal charge for lessons. I began with the clarinet, reached the point where I could play an elementary tune on it, and then lost interest. Next, I took up the trombone, learned to do an imitation of an automobile horn, and gave up on that. I moved on to the baritone horn but decided that it sounded foolish. Finally I tried the trumpet, and that stuck. I took trumpet lessons in Rochester and worked fairly hard, and when we moved to New York I continued the lessons with a nice man named Edmund Treutel, who taught at the Ninety-second Street Young Men's Hebrew Association. Because there was a large pool at the Y, I could combine a trumpet lesson with the thirty-odd laps I swam daily for practice.

Mr. Treutel was a classical trumpet player, so I studied classical trumpet, which meant, in those days, working through the Arban book of trumpet exercises. Finding a place to practice was a problem. My brother and I shared a room in the back of our apartment that looked over a large air shaft — or small courtyard, depending on how one viewed it — with wonderful acoustics. But after the neighbors complained, I got a mute. When I discovered Harry James, that was the end of my interest in the classical trumpet; I was going to teach myself to play jazz. James, who was at the height of his celebrity, lived a few buildings south of us on Central Park West. I wrote him a note offering to set up music stands, if necessary, in order to learn from the master. I got back a very kind postcard from the manager of the orchestra, Frank Monte, saying, "We already have a man to set up the stands"; he added, "The best of luck with your trumpet and just practice as long as you can." By the time I got this card it was all but irrelevant, for I had begun a friendship with Duke Ellington and several members of his orchestra that was to last several years.

This very significant aspect of my high school life requires some explanation. When I was a sophomore at Columbia Grammar I began writing a column for the school newspaper. The column, which I called "Seeing Stars," consisted of interviews that I arranged with well-known show people who came through New York. Our newspaper issued some sort of a press card; armed with it, and a good deal of nerve, I managed to interview Tommy Dorsey, Edgar Bergen, Benny Goodman, Henry Morgan, and others. I have a vivid recollection of my interview with Morgan, which I had arranged by phone. When I showed up at his suite in one of the hotels overlooking Central Park on Fifty-ninth Street, he was somewhat taken aback. He had assumed that the *Columbia News* was a publication of Columbia University and did not expect to be interrogated by a high school sophomore. I, in turn, did not expect him to be an intellectual and was surprised to see a living room table covered with serious-looking books. I asked, in all innocence, whether he actually read those books. He said no, he did not, but that "the table was filled with helium and he had the books on it to weigh it down because otherwise it had a tendency to fly up and stick to the ceiling." I duly reported this in my column.

Many of my interviews were conducted in the radio studios — the NBC Red and Blue Network studios — in Radio City, at 30 Rockefeller Plaza. On those rare weekdays when I didn't have football or swimming practice, and often on the weekends, I would take the AA train from Central Park West to Radio City and haunt the studios, looking for people to interview and generally enjoying the ambience. It was on one of those Saturdays that I discovered Duke Ellington and his orchestra.

I had wandered into a large studio where a number of musicians were sitting around with their instruments casually laid out beside them. I sat down and waited to see what would happen. A few minutes before four o'clock an announcer came on stage, and precisely at four a piano player appeared. I later found out that it was Billy Strayhorn. He began a solo opening chorus — those chords which became almost the anthem for my high school years — and then from all sides of the studio the musicians got up from their chairs and played the beginning of "Take the 'A' Train" while they walked to the stage. I was completely stunned by both the music and the musicians and, I am afraid, instantly abandoned

Harry James. "The Flight of the Bumblebee" — one of James's virtuoso shticks on the trumpet — seemed pretty trivial compared with what Cootie Williams could do with a plunger mute. Having made this glorious discovery, I was determined to come back every Saturday and get to know these superlative musicians well enough to write about them in my column. My chance came on the third or fourth visit, when I noticed two of the musicians playing chess. I had had a few lessons with Hertzberger and had read a couple of chess books, and after watching the game for a little while, I saw that it was a classic case of *potzerism*. I didn't say anything, but when one of the musicians left, the other asked whether I would like to play. It was an adolescent fantasy come true. We played several games while members of the orchestra gathered around, making sarcastic comments at the expense of my opponent, Al Sears, the tenor saxophone player who had replaced the great Ben Webster. Sears, whom I got to know pretty well over the years, had two personalities. Off-stage he was a quiet, studious man given to chess playing and pipe smoking; on-stage, he was a wild man. Some of the rest of Ellington's sidemen had a difficult time putting up with his performing personality, and when Sears really got smoking on stage, they would pass around one of those metal trumpet mutes shaped like a hat. As the hat came by, each musician, with a loud clank, would toss in a handful of small change — a joke that did not amuse Mr. Ellington at all.

Sears had just written a jazz piece called "Castle Rock," and I was puzzled about the etymology of the title. "You see, Jerry," he explained carefully, "a rock is a [sexually explicit noun], and a Castle Rock is a great big [sexually explicit noun]." At the time I had not had a [sexually explicit noun), but I recorded the information in my notebook.

Sears introduced me to all the members of the orchestra: Johnny Hodges, the magnificent alto saxophone player who was known as Rabbit; Harry Carney, a deeply religious man who played a great baritone saxophone and really anchored the orchestra; trumpet players like Ray Nance, "the man who dance"; drummer Sonny Greer, who seemed to be in a world of his own; and Al Hibbler, the blind singer. Apart from Sears, my closest friend became William Alonzo Anderson, known as Cat because of his feline appearance. A short, very powerful man with the broad face of a large cat, he was noted for his trumpet solos featuring soaring high notes. He was soft-spoken and immensely kind. When I finally worked up the courage to tell him that I played the trumpet, he insisted that I bring it down to the studio so that he could hear me. I was, in truth, a very mediocre trumpet player, but Cat was generous enough to give me some hints, especially about playing jazz. The apprenticeship reached its high point when Cat — probably with the permission of Duke Ellington — let me sit in with him during a gig that the band had at the old Hurricane Club on Broadway. I blew a few notes and felt very grand.

I got to know Duke Ellington as well. I have no idea who he thought I was or what I was doing there — *there* being everywhere in the New York metropolitan area where the band was playing — but it was obvious that I was full of admiration and good will. I wrote an affectionate and admiring column about him for the school paper. Several years later, when I was in college but was visiting my parents in Rochester, the orchestra came to Batavia, New York, to play an engagement. I am not sure that Cat

Anderson was with it then. He had tried to go it on his own several times, and on one occasion I even tried — in vain — to get financing for him from Nat King Cole, whom I had also interviewed for my column. Al Sears stayed at our house in Rochester. My father had never met Duke Ellington and was not, to put it mildly, much of a jazz fan. However, he agreed to drive us to Batavia and, indeed, to stay and listen to the concert. Sears thought that my father and Duke Ellington should meet, so he arranged for the four of us to have lunch together, at a restaurant named the Berry Patch. All the décor was in berries of one kind or another. My father and Ellington had a pleasant talk, during which Ellington asked my father what he would take to a desert island if he could take only two things, adding that he would take the Bible and Lena Horne. I don't remember my father's choices.

During the first year I hung around the orchestra, my parents did not pay much attention. By the time I was a senior in high school, I was really spending a lot of time with it, including nights when I would go to Harlem or midtown New York, and then I was not under parental supervision at all. In 1946 President Truman made my father a special assistant to General Joseph T. McNarney, commander of the remaining American forces in Europe. My father was to aid in resettling the 200,000 displaced Jews, largely from Central and Eastern Europe, who were the last survivors of the Jewish population of that region. Most of them had been in concentration camps and did not want to — or could not — return to their native countries. It is sometimes forgotten that after the war there were pogroms in Poland; my father helped the army deal with the refugees from these postwar anti-Semitic outbreaks. His headquarters were in Frankfurt, with the headquarters of the United States armed forces in Europe.

So, at the end of my junior year in high school the rest of the family left for Germany. My parents felt that disrupting my education might make it difficult for me to get into college. This was a time when colleges were overcrowded, because returning soldiers were joining newly graduated high school students, and the competition for admission was very intense. Being left in New York suited me just fine. My plumbing-fixture-manufacturing grandfather owned a brownstone off Central Park West some blocks north of my school. He and my grandmother lived on one floor; on the floor below was a cousin; and on two floors above lived my biochemist uncle and his wife and family. There was a spare room on the first floor of their apartment, and it became mine. I had my own key; there were no rules; I came and went as I pleased. I was doing reasonably well in school and seemed healthy enough, so no one asked any questions about what I did when I was away from the house. I wasn't really doing anything that unusual, apart from spending a few nights a week in Harlem or elsewhere listening to jazz. When I went to Harlem, Cat Anderson or Al Sears would see to it that I didn't get into trouble. And that's how I happily spent my senior year — absorbing jazz, playing football, swimming, and column writing.

One may wonder where in all of this was the science? The answer is, nowhere. My mother has saved my report cards all the way back to the 1930s, and I defy anyone looking at this curious record to predict that the child was to become a physicist. I showed ability in things like "oral English," an eighth-grade subject whose precise content eludes me. For the year 1939–1940, which must have been at the height of my grasshopper phase, my teacher,

Miss F. H. Calbout, noted, "Jeremy seems to have taken more interest in his work." The use of the word "seems" tells all. According to Miss Calbout, the only subject I demonstrated any special ability in was reading. In all of high school I took one science course, and it made so little impression on me that until I looked through the collection of report cards, I could not remember whether it was chemistry, physics, or biology. It turned out to have been physics, in which I got a class grade of 75, my lowest grade by far in anything that semester. I do remember the teacher, Mr. Randel, a very kind man who, I believe, had been an equipment demonstrator in a department store before he became our science teacher. I have no idea what his training in science was, but I doubt it would have made the slightest difference in my case. My teacher could have been Richard Feynman himself and it wouldn't have mattered. I wasn't interested.

There was a mathematics club run by a sulfurous mathematics teacher named Mr. Reynolds, a club, needless to say, that I did not join. Mr. Reynolds had high standards and kept comparing us with earlier students like Murray Gell-Mann. After making the comparison, he would add, "In Tarrytown [where he lived] we bury our dead," a reference to the poor lot he was then confronted with. As far as I was concerned, mathematics was a series of exercises and puzzles that had no purpose other than to lead to a final examination. That it was a real subject with intellectual content and beauty I had no inkling. In fact, I think that in some profound sense I had no intellectual interests at all.

Yet it was a foregone conclusion that I would go to college. If anyone had asked me why, I probably would have answered that everyone in our family goes to college. Nor would it have occurred to me how wrong this observation was. Before my father's generation few if any of my family had had a higher education, and most of the women of my father's generation, and some of the men, had no higher education either. Mine was the first generation for which going to college was a given. But what college? Columbia Grammar had a very good college adviser, Mr. Hugh Merson. To this day I think of him with affection and respect. He signed my report cards with statements like "Promoted to the High School. Hugh Merson. Director gr 5–8. Good luck to the freshman!" He looks out at me from my high school yearbook as straight and clear as a brook. I don't know how much of my life I shared with him, but he must have known I was on my own during my senior year, and he certainly read my columns. I think he really felt I might be able to get everything together and make something of my life, and he encouraged me to apply to the best colleges, even though my academic record was somewhat mixed.

On the subject of colleges the counsel was diverse. There were those who said I should be a big fish in a small pond, and there were those who said I should be a small fish in a big pond. The small-pond people said I should go to Swarthmore, so I duly spent a weekend at Swarthmore. There was a track meet, and after one of the events, in which a Swarthmore man placed somewhere, a group of girls came out of the stands and put a laurel wreath on his brow. I decided on the spot that this was not the place for me. Too "kissy," as Duke Ellington would have put it. I had visited Syracuse many times with my father, and in view of his connection, I applied there. An uncle who had done graduate work at Harvard said that he found it socially uncomfortable, but he had been there in the 1930s, when the club system, which was inhospitable to Jews and other minorities, was in full swing. On the other hand, I thought, Harvard was at least in a city; moreover, my best friend, Henry Steiner, had applied and was certain to get in. So I applied there, even though Mr. Merson had warned me that it was unlikely that our small private school — my graduating class consisted of forty-eight students — would have two acceptances from Harvard.

As expected, Henry was accepted by Harvard, and on May 26, 1947, I received word that I had been accepted, too. I decided to give the big pond a try. It transformed my life. If this needs any proof, all I have to do is to look at my senior yearbook. In many ways this is the strangest souvenir I have of my childhood and youth. The forty-eight of us stare out of the pages looking "our best." Under our names are captions that are supposed to tell something of our character. Henry Steiner's caption is "Hail to the Chief." (Henry was the editor of the newspaper for two years.) Others had captions like "Body and Soul," "Personality," and "You Keep Coming Back Like a Song." Under my picture is "Young Man with a Horn." There are prophecies made for the year 1967, twenty years after our graduation. Most of them contain references to school gossip whose significance I no longer know. They were written with a nasty edge that obviously was meant to pass for wit. The prophecy about Henry Steiner reads, in part, "I read the latest *Police Gazette*, owned and edited by Henry Steiner." In 1967 Henry Steiner was a professor at the Harvard Law School. The first part of my prophecy reads, "I heard the other day from Jerry (Blimpo) Bernstein, the new arranger for the black-blue rhythms of Rastus Keller." By 1967 I had been working as a professional physicist for over a decade.

3

The River

IT WAS September of 1947. I was seventeen and had been in Cambridge for about two weeks. I was homesick. On second thought, "homesick" doesn't seem exactly the right word. I had not been living at *home* for over a year. What I missed was not so much home but New York — the jazz, Broadway, and, above all, the food.

By this time I had managed to lose the forty-odd pounds of flab. During some of my summers in high school I had gone to a camp in Maine that had some relationship to Columbia Grammar; many of the Kamp Kohut counselors taught at the school. My brother had had a counselor named Ben Hammer, who played college football. He must have learned from Stephen that I played high school football, so he came to see me. He took one look and said, "You are a blivet." A blivet was defined as ten pounds of manure in a five-pound sack. Ben said that he was about to go into training for the fall football season, and offered to take me and another blivet, Fred Bernard, also a football player, and run us until the fat came off. He did. Up and down we ran, then into the water to swim laps, then more running, then push-ups and sit-ups until we were ready to drop. I was too tired to eat, and by the time I returned to school for my senior year I was almost unrecognizable. But I still loved food, especially the kind found in those marvelous places on the Upper West Side, like Barney Greengrass — "the Sturgeon King" — and the Tip Toe Inn, which featured a banana cream pie the thought of which makes my mouth water even now, forty years later.

Now for the first time in my life I was confronted with dormitory food. It was not bad, despite the rumor that on Friday nights the meat course featured animals who had died during the week in the Boston zoo. But it had no character. We stood in a long line while thin Irish girls from South Boston ladled portions of slightly watery spinach from vats onto our trays. I felt very sorry for the girls, and for one in particular, who looked especially unhappy and whom I tried to cheer up as I waited in line. I must have made some sort of impression on her, because years later when I took a plane from New York to Boston there she was, a stewardess, and she remembered me from the long line.

One Sunday, after about two weeks of the line, I decided to try to forage in greater Cambridge. I was by myself and was missing New York. It was a lovely autumn night, and as I was walking along Massachusetts Avenue, nursing my melancholy, I spotted what appeared, from the outside, to be a delicatessen. Inside, there was a counter with stools, and I said to the proprietor, somewhat pointlessly, "Can people eat at the counter?" "Sonny," he answered with an accent, "what do you think they're doing there?" I could have embraced the man, more so after consuming an inspiriting portion of cheese blintzes topped off with a generous slice of cheese cake, the kind that now causes a twinge in my coronary arteries. I walked back slowly to Harvard Yard with the certain feeling that I would get through the semester.

During the previous year Richard Gummere, who was chairman of the Committee on Admissions at Harvard, had written to my father in Germany to alert him to the difficulties of admission to Harvard that coming semester and the unusually large size of the expected freshman class. One effect of this situation was that the housing was more crowded than usual, with students from different classes jumbled together. I lived with three other students, including Henry Steiner, in a small suite of rooms in Matthews Hall that would have accommodated two or three of us in more normal circumstances. The first thing that struck me about this kind of dormitory living was that there were rules. I don't think that they were very Draconian; they involved things like visitation hours. But nonetheless they were clearly stated and prominently posted. This seemed a step backward to me; after all, I had been on my own in New York for over a year. The rules were administered by a proctor. In Matthews, the proctor was a young law student named Richard Kleindienst, later the attorney general of the United States under Richard Nixon. I don't remember much about him except that he spoke with what seemed to me an odd accent — he was from Arizona. Like all law students, he was drowning in work.

Fortunately, as a freshman I had very little choice in my courses. There was an English composition requirement, so I enrolled in English composition. There was a "humanities" requirement, so I enrolled in a huge general-education course taught by I. A. Richards. And then there was the science requirement. If it had not been for this requirement, I never would have become a physicist — and that is why I say the lack of choice was fortunate.

There was also a swimming requirement. Harvard required every undergraduate to demonstrate the ability to swim two laps of a twenty-five-yard pool. For the four years of my high school life I swam some thirty laps a day, five days a week, five months a year, and I had decided when I graduated never willingly to enter a chlorinated swimming pool again. However, I was quite willing to swim the two laps needed to graduate, and I completed that requirement shortly after term began. I also had some notion that I might try out for freshman football. To this end I went to the field house across the Charles River, where the teams assembled, to size up the situation. As I was walking to the field house, I passed a football field in which some behemoths were practicing. At first I thought they were the Boston professional team, but they were wearing Harvard uniforms. When, on inquiring, I was told that they were *freshmen* — a specially invited group of freshmen — here for presemester practice, I decided that college football was not for me. Then I thought of going out for crew, but soon realized I was too short. Still, I loved being on the river, and during the nearly ten years I eventually spent at Harvard, I went rowing whenever I could.

When I entered Harvard my determination not to take any more science courses ran a close second to my strong feelings about not getting into swimming pools. But there was that science requirement. On closer examination I saw that general-education courses in science were offered in various subjects at various levels. Finding your level was something like joining classes in a ski school.

Further inquiry convinced me that the lowest possible level was Natural Sciences 3, taught by I. Bernard Cohen, the historian of science. This course, it was said, was for people who were basket cases in science. That sounded just right for me. Cohen turned out to be an ample, comfortable man with magnificent handwriting. There was something pleasantly reassuring about the way he wrote the formulae; they had round, nonthreatening shapes. He drew beautiful diagrams, and the classroom demonstrations were entertaining and equally nonthreatening.

The course began with the ancient Greeks and Egyptians. We learned Aristarchus of Samos' argument for finding the distance of the sun from the earth, and Eratosthenes' argument, which gave him very nearly the correct circumference of the earth. We moved through the Middle Ages and on to Copernicus, Kepler, and Galileo. Cohen was a Newton scholar, so we spent a good deal of time on Newton. The course then turned to chemists like Robert Boyle, who contributed to the atomic theory of matter, and then back to the nineteenth-century physicists like Michael Faraday and James Clerk Maxwell, who created the modern theory of electromagnetism. We scattered bits of iron filings in the neighborhood of an electromagnet and mapped the field lines, the way Faraday had done. Cohen displayed the method by which J. J. Thomson, at the end of the nineteenth century, discovered the electron. None of this involved any mathematics beyond the high school mathematics at which I had been fairly proficient, and none of it was of sufficient interest to me to have turned me into a physicist. Then came relativity.

I no longer remember how Cohen introduced relativity. He certainly told us that the mass of the electron increased with its velocity and that rulers shrank. I found both of these revelations absolutely mind-boggling. As I look back on it now I am hard put to say exactly why. After all, until I took Cohen's course I knew nothing about electrons. Why should I have been surprised that their mass increased as they went faster, especially since I did not know, before taking the course, what mass was? It is an example of how deeply embedded certain common-sense ideas are. Even though a nonphysicist has only the vaguest notion of what mass is, a *variable* mass still seems like an oxymoron. These revelations really caught my attention, especially when Cohen said — possibly as a joke, although I took it seriously — that only nine, or twelve, people in the world understood the theory of relativity. I forget whether he included himself. Years later I discovered that this was a take-off on the celebrated colloquy involving the British astronomer Sir Arthur Eddington, whose early book on relativity (the one Robert Oppenheimer recommended to his brother) is still a classic. Asked if it was true that only three people in the world understood relativity, he thought for a minute and replied, "Who is the third?" In any event I decided, with the bravado characteristic of a Harvard freshman, that I would become the tenth, or thirteenth, person to understand relativity.

Fortunately I did not mention this plan to anybody. If I had, I would no doubt have been told that any competent graduate student in physics understands at least some of the theory and that, given my background, I didn't have a chance in the world of understanding it. Either of these observations would have stopped me in my tracks. But now I was armed with a secret ambition. So I went off to Widener Library to see whether it happened to have a book on relativity. I decided that I might as well start with a work by Einstein, since he, at least, must have understood the theory. There were two books. One was called simply *Relativity* and the other was *The Meaning of Relativity*. I liked the sound of the second title, so I checked it out. It was the wrong choice. It could not have been a worse choice. But it took me a while to find that out. *The Meaning of Relativity* is a collection of lectures Einstein delivered in Princeton in 1921 to an audience of physicists. From my point of view the great advantage of the book was its size; the main text is only 108 pages. I reasoned that I would read one page a day and at that rate would have mastered the book in a little over three months. I thought of approaching the matter in somewhat the way we learned poems such as Scott's *The Lady of the Lake* in high school. I would memorize certain passages so that I could repeat them to myself until I thoroughly understood them. Surely I could understand anything written in English if only I read it slowly.

The book begins straightforwardly enough. "The theory of relativity is intimately connected with the theory of space and time," Einstein writes. So far so good. He then describes the experience of time and what is understood by a clock. Thus endeth page one. For five days I proceeded with my plan, if not understanding everything, at least understanding enough to feel encouraged. On the sixth day the whole thing collapsed. In the middle of the page there stood a formula of which I could understand nothing. The symbols were completely meaningless to me. It was not going to be like reading *The Lady of the Lake* after all. I did not know what to do, so I went to speak to Cohen. I was afraid that he might ridicule the whole idea, but, in fact, he made what turned out to be one of those suggestions that can change a person's life. He said that the physics department was offering a spring-semester course, Physics 16, that concerned itself with philosophical and historical questions of modern science, most particularly the theory of relativity. It was being taught, he said, by Philipp Frank — a name that meant nothing to me — and that Professor Frank was a friend of Einstein's. *That* meant something. The course was normally open only to sophomores who had had the equivalent of his Natural Sciences 3, but that there would probably be no objection if I took Physics 16 and the second half of his course concurrently. Nothing ventured, nothing gained. I enrolled in Physics 16.

The course was scheduled to meet late on Wednesday afternoons in the large lecture hall in the Jefferson Physics Laboratory. I found the room pretty full, for Professor Frank's course attracted scholars from many departments. I took my place toward the rear of the hall and waited. A few minutes after the hour, he walked in, limping slightly — years later I learned that his injury had resulted from a childhood encounter with a streetcar in Vienna, where Professor Frank was born in 1884 — and put an ancient-looking set of notes on the large lecture table. He was a short, somewhat oval man, largely devoid of hair. What hair he did have floated, in white wisps, in various directions, as if in a breeze. Without meaning any disrespect, I can describe his face as resembling that of an exceedingly intelligent basset hound. The corners of his mouth were turned up in an expectant smile. In later years, when I would talk for hours with Professor Frank, I learned that it was very important that I not say anything during this latent smile phase. The expression signaled that Professor Frank was recalling the details of what was often an extremely funny anecdote; if I interrupted the process, the anecdote would get lost. On the opening day of class, the anecdote concerned some Cambridge urchins who had fired on Professor Frank with a few snowballs. During the not very damaging assault one of them had announced that he was from the "fourth dimension," which proved, Professor Frank observed, just how deeply Einstein's ideas had penetrated popular culture.

This tale was told in an extraordinary English accent. After thinking about it for several years — and after learning that Frank was fluent in German, French, Italian, Spanish, Russian, Czech, and English, and was able to read Persian, Arabic, Hebrew, Latin, and Greek — I decided that each of the spoken languages had been laid on top of the preceding one, like the successive cities of Troy. English was the topmost language, but the other ones, buried underneath, sometimes obtruded themselves during Professor Frank's conversation. He once explained to me the politics of studying English in the middle 1930s at the German University in Prague, where he had succeeded Einstein in 1912. The existence of the German University was a consequence of the decision by the Austrian government in 1888 to split the existing university linguistically because of the interminable quarrels between the German- and Czech-speaking professors. Professor Frank used to tell a story about two German-speaking professors. While walking down the street, one noticed a sign that was about to fall onto the sidewalk. The other said, "It doesn't much matter. If it falls, it's likely to hit a Czech." In the 1930s there was a group at the university, described by Frank as the "Nazis," who lived in fear that the Russians would invade Czechoslovakia and put them in prison. Then there were the "Communists," who were afraid that the Germans would invade and put them in prison, and finally there were the Jews, who were sure that invasion by either would be a disaster for them. The only thing that the three groups could agree on, Frank told me, was the necessity to hire a teacher to teach them English so that they could all emigrate to the United States.

I still have the notes from Professor Frank's lectures, and I use them when I teach the theory of relativity, especially to undergraduates who have a minimum of mathematics. In the course he taught us that spring of 1948, relativity was not discussed until we were well into the subject matter. We began with a discussion of the logic of geometry. Professor Frank wanted to make sure we understood the distinction between geometry as a series of statements about the physical world that could be tested experimentally, and geometry as a system of logic that could not be refuted as long as it was internally consistent. This is crucial to an understanding of how there can be non-Euclidean geometries that are logically consistent but appear to defy common sense. For example, in non-Euclidean geometries there can be *many* lines drawn through a point that are parallel to a given line. These geometries may or may not have anything to do with the real world, depending on what the real world turns out to be.

We then studied the history of the relativity principle, which in its modern form can be traced back at least as far as Galileo. Galileo was convinced that the laws of physics would be the same for someone on the deck of a ship moving smoothly and uniformly through the water as for a person on land, something that we now call the Galilean relativity principle, a term that I believe was coined by Professor Frank. Next, Frank described the development of the theories of light leading up to the attempt by Albert Michelson and Edward Morley in 1887 to measure — unsuccessfully — the velocity of the earth through the putative "luminiferous aether."

I had no real standard of comparison by which to assess the quality of Professor Frank's explanation. All I knew was that I understood, or thought I understood, what he was talking about. The lectures seemed very clear to me while I was listening to them. After class I would walk from the Jefferson Laboratory to my room in Matthews Hall and try to reconstruct them for myself. It was only then that I realized how subtle they were and how much effort was required on my part to understand them. This was especially true of Professor Frank's discussion of Einstein's theory of relativity, which proceeded from the operational definitions of space and time, in terms of measurements with clocks and rulers, to the ways in which these measurements were compared when the observers were in motion with respect to each other — which leads to the transformation equations of relativity. The lectures were always divided in two parts, separated by what Frank characterized as a "certain interval." After the interval — usually ten minutes — we had a question period. It was at this time that Professor Frank revealed the full range of his erudition. On one memorable occasion, he wrote down a quotation from an obscure author in Persian, a language he had studied decades earlier in Vienna.

But the most impressive aspect of the course was the mathematics. According to the ground rules, no higher mathematics was drawn on during the first hour, which covered the material we were responsible for. Some of the questions that came up after the interval, however, were best answered by reference to mathematics like the calculus. Professor Frank would always preface these answers by saying to the questioner, "If you know a little of mathematics . . ." It became increasingly clear to me that I would never progress beyond the dilettante state unless I learned "a little of mathematics."

I had no intention of becoming a professional mathematician, still less a professional physicist. I had been to Professor Frank's office several times and found the general atmosphere of the physics department — populated by what seemed to me to be shadowy drones armed with two-foot slide rules — gloomy and intimidating. In fact, I had absolutely no idea what I was going to be or even what I was going to major in. I did want to study further with Professor Frank and I did want to understand relativity on a deeper level, and I knew that I could do so only if I learned some higher mathematics. A few freshmen I met had taken the calculus and found it very difficult; it is a kind of watershed in one's mathematical education. I decided that I had better have my freshman adviser look up my mathematical aptitude tests to see whether I had the wit to learn the calculus. I suppose if he had reported back that my test scores were low, I would have given up. But he said they were quite adequate, so I no longer had an excuse not to enroll in the first-year calculus course as a sophomore. I was also able to take a reading course in the philosophy of science with Professor Frank. It was a little unusual for a sophomore to take a reading course, but the great thing about Harvard was that you could take almost any course if you could give a sensible reason.

During my undergraduate years at Harvard I had the good fortune to run into a small number of influential teachers, Philipp Frank being the first, and the second being the mathematician George Mackey, whose elementary calculus course I enrolled in for my sophomore year. In time, Mackey became for a small group of my mathematically inclined contemporaries at Harvard not exactly a father figure, since Mackey was not that much older than we were, but a sort of legend. Mackey stories abounded. He was, when I knew him then, totally devoted to mathematics; he was a mathematical monk of a singularly amiable and benign variety. He lived in a suite in one of the Harvard Houses and was always at work on two or three problems simultaneously. Mackey was wholly honest and forthcoming. On one occasion, he told us, he had dreamed that he had *become* a "partial derivative," something that we tried, for weeks, to analyze.

As a teacher, Mackey was the antithesis of Cohen. It was not that Mackey's lectures were not prepared. In fact his notes, especially for the more advanced courses, often circulated as texts. It was, I think, that considerable time elapsed between the preparation of the notes and the time they were delivered. I tend to work the same way, although when preparing a new course I do write the whole thing out in advance to put the structure in perspective. I suspect Mackey did the same. But by the time I give the actual lectures, I have forgotten, unless I have written them out carefully, the detailed arguments for various elementary steps, and unless I can figure them out on the spot I get stuck — which, I am sure, gives my students a great deal of satisfaction. This used to happen frequently to Mackey. When it did, he would turn red with embarrassment and smile with a sort of amiable futility. On one occasion he said he thought he had the proof in his notes, but when he looked, all he found was

"The proof of this theorem is trivial." Mackey read that to us with a puzzled grin. There were usually enough sharpshooters in the class so that one of the students could see the trouble and get Mackey started again. If not, Mackey would assign the offending theorem as a problem. All of his courses, from the most elementary to the most advanced, were entirely original and very deep. The Harvard "Confi Guide," that fount of student wisdom on courses and teachers, reported that Mackey "talked too fast and wrote illegibly, according to one student." There was, no doubt, some truth to this, but it was also beside the point.

Meanwhile, my musical life was proceeding after a fashion. I joined the Harvard-Radcliffe Symphony Orchestra as the nth trumpet. Its conductor was the eminent Malcolm Holmes, composer of, among other pieces, "The Musical Clock," often played by the Boston Pops. Most of the members of the orchestra were serious musicians, which I was not, and there was an inner circle of them known as the Pierian Sodality. Once in a while the rest of us were allowed to share the activities of the elite; one such occasion stands out vividly in my mind. We had given a concert in Sanders Theatre in Cambridge. At the afterconcert party in some local restaurant, the Pierians were clustered around Holmes while we lesser folk were banished to the far reaches of the room. To add to my general feeling of discontent, the ill-fitting collar of my rented tuxedo was so tight that it had made a small cut on my neck, which began to bleed onto the shirt. I felt like John the Baptist. I had had a few glasses of wine and had reached the point where I knew that, if pressed, I might say something really interesting. Just then, the

Pierians presented Holmes with an unfortunate small live turtle bearing the conductor's name painted on its back. Groping for something to say, Holmes quipped, "If it gets any bigger, I'll have to sell it." I then heard a peculiar voice that seemed to come from me saying, "If it gets any bigger, it will sell you." There was a general silence punctuated with nervous laughter from Holmes. Feeling it was time to leave, I made my way uncertainly out into the snowy night. It was the last Pierian party I attended.

Concurrent with this classical musical activity was the meteoric rise and fall of the New Friends of Jazz, an entity that I created out of whole cloth in the fall of 1948. It was dedicated, in the words from "The Old Dope Peddler," by my Harvard contemporary Tom Lehrer, to "doing well by doing good." My idea was to form what might pass as a club, whose purpose was to bring jazz to the Harvard campus and would make us money in the process. I therefore composed the following document, which twelve of us signed and sent to whatever Harvard authorities were responsible for the formation of clubs:

> Sirs:
>
> The interest in jazz expressed by most Americans is as pronounced at Harvard as elsewhere. However, in the recent past there has been no group at the college which was willing to take the initiative in organizing, sponsoring, and presenting the best in modern jazz via the concert stage. We of the New Friends of Jazz hope to fill this gap.
>
> The New Friends of Jazz proposes to present a series of four concerts in Sander's Theatre during the following year. The first of these is tentatively planned for November 12 and will feature Duke Ellington and his orchestra. We plan to charge an ad-

mission sufficiently great so that Mr. Ellington and his successors will be able to play the date without financial loss to themselves. Further, we wish to make sufficient money to enable us to run our organization in the future on a sound basis.

As the New Friends is purely a promotional unit, the ordinary mechanism of club government is unnecessary. The members have been selected for particular talents and will each have an area of responsibility in which he will have complete charge. Policy decisions will be made by simple majority vote and for the time being Jerry Bernstein and Sidney Stires have assumed the offices of president and vice president.

S. Homer (Sidney) Stires, now a successful New York investment banker, was a classmate and an excellent stride pianist.

I had gone so far as to get a commitment from Duke Ellington to come to Boston on the eve of Armistice Day and had hired the Rindge Technical High School auditorium near the campus. We even had tickets printed, ranging from $2.40 to $1.20. At this point the university stepped in and decided that as this was apparently a commercial enterprise, we could not be a club. We all got cold feet, the concert was canceled, and that is the last that was ever heard from the New Friends of Jazz.

That fall I also began my reading course with Professor Frank. Our idea was to read together a certain number of the classics in the philosophy of science. We began with Aristotle and progressed into the Middle Ages, reading philosophers like Aquinas and William of Occam. We read some Hume, Locke, and Mill, but concentrated mostly on the positivists, such as Comte, Stallo, Charles Sanders Peirce, and, above all, Ernst Mach. Professor

Frank had had some contact with Mach in Vienna and in a certain sense had been Mach's heir at the German University in Prague. Mach had been a professor there and was rector from 1867 to 1895, when he returned to Vienna, where he had taken his doctorate. In 1912 Professor Frank arranged a meeting between Mach and Einstein, with whom he had been in contact since 1907. Mach disbelieved in the "existence" — the reality — of atoms, and Einstein's early scientific career was devoted to the statistical mechanics of large assemblies of atoms. Neither man succeeded in changing the other's mind.

Professor Frank also told me something of his own intellectual life. He had been a physics student in Vienna and had studied with Ludwig Boltzmann, among others. Boltzmann was one of the founders of the discipline of statistical mechanics and one of Einstein's predecessors. He and Mach often argued about the atomic hypothesis — the question of whether or not atoms exist. Mach's favorite question to Boltzmann concerning atoms was "Have you seen one?" Boltzmann committed suicide in 1906 and it has been said that a proximate cause was his disagreements with Mach. Professor Frank thought that this was nonsense and pointed out that, apart from the matter of the atoms, Boltzmann considered himself a philosophical disciple of Mach's. I once asked Professor Frank who was the most impressive mathematical physicist he had ever met. I thought he would answer Einstein, but he said it was Boltzmann. The young Einstein, he told me, was much given to jokes and to what Professor Frank referred to as "cracks."

Early in his career, even when he was writing papers in mathematical physics, Professor Frank's main interest was in the philosophy of science. In 1907 he and a small group of equally brilliant young men began meeting every Thursday night in one of the old Viennese coffee houses to discuss the connection between philosophy and science. They tried to learn everything. One of their number, the economist Otto Neurath, even enrolled for a year in the divinity school of the University of Vienna to learn Catholic philosophy; he won a prize for the best paper on moral theology. In 1929 the group decided to become a movement, and Neurath invented the name Vienna Circle, because, as Professor Frank once wrote, "he thought that this name would be reminiscent of the Viennese waltz, the Vienna woods, and other things on the pleasant side of life." The philosophy the group expounded became known as logical positivism; it was an attempt to rid the interpretation of science of what Professor Frank used to refer to as "school philosophy" — raw metaphysics.

The circle had common interests with the logicians Ludwig Wittgenstein and Bertrand Russell, both of whom Professor Frank had known. As part of our reading course we read Wittgenstein's *Tractatus Logico-Philosophicus*, with alternating pages of English and German that Professor Frank would search for linguistic nuances. The Vienna group also had common interests with the physicist Percy Bridgman, who had introduced the notion of "operational definitions" — defining such terms as "field," "space," and "time" by specifying the methods needed to measure them. We read Bridgman's book *The Logic of Modern Physics* and, because Bridgman had been a member of the Harvard physics faculty since 1908 and was still active, we discussed parts of the book with him. My first published paper was a consequence of this interaction. It was a brief critical account of some of the aspects of Bridgman's philosophy, which Professor Frank arranged to be published in the Dutch journal *Synthese*. After reading it, Bridgman called me into his basement laboratory to debate some of the points I had made. My only certain recollection of this discussion was Bridgman's remark that as a "critic" I had treated him more kindly than many. I don't know whether he realized that I was nineteen. He had won the Nobel Prize in Physics in 1946, the year before I entered Harvard.

Bridgman was such an iconoclast, Professor Frank once told me, that when his daughter got married, Bridgman, who believed in no form of religion, had the governor of Massachusetts make him a justice of the peace for a day so that he could perform the marriage ceremony himself.

One of the crazier notions I got during my sophomore year was that I should visit Einstein in Princeton to discuss the philosophy of relativity with him. Looking back, I am embarrassed by the whole notion. I had not yet had a single proper course in physics and had had only one course in mathematics. But I had a lot of nerve. And Professor Frank, who had just written his splendid biography, *Einstein, His Life and Times*, was making fairly regular visits to Princeton. He must have brought up the subject of my going to Princeton, because just after the close of the spring term of that year I received the following letter, in English:

> Dear Mr. Bernstein:
>
> I am sending you enclosed a paper in which I expressed opinions from an epistological [*sic*] point of view. I do not give oral interviews to avoid misinterpretations.
>
> Sincerely yours,
> A. Einstein

The paper was "Physics and Reality," and I have the copy he sent me, although by now it is worn thin from my many readings.

During the course of that year I got to visit Professor Frank and his wife, Hania, fairly often. The walls of their small, comfortable apartment near Harvard Square were covered with photographs of Professor Frank with assorted dignitaries. Hania, who had been a student of Professor Frank's in Prague, was a character in her own right. She often made fun of her husband's lack of interest in the arts. She had been a member of the circle in Prague that included Kafka, and she once told me that she did not then think that Kafka was as gifted a writer as some of the other young writers she knew. Both she and Professor Frank tried to preserve some facets of their European university life, Mrs. Frank by belonging to several cultural groups in Cambridge. I have an indelible memory of calling the apartment once and of Mrs. Frank's saying, in a very thick accent, "We are here singing English folk songs and Philipp has gone away." He could usually be found in the nearby Hayes Bickford cafeteria, which took the place for him of one of his beloved Viennese coffee houses. We had many discussions over cups of coffee in the Hayes Bickford. The Franks had originally come to this country in 1938 for a lecture tour, in which Professor Frank spoke at something like twenty universities. When the war broke out, in 1939, Harvard found him a half-time lectureship. He earned the rest of his living from guest professorships and his writing, and he and Hania lived very modestly.

By the end of my sophomore year I still was uncertain about what I would major in. The only thing that was clear was that one course in mathematics was not nearly enough to bring me to some understanding of Einstein's relativity book. I decided that I had better stay in Cambridge over the summer and take more mathematics. Professor Frank gave me a job collecting material for some research he was doing on how intellectuals in different countries reacted to Einstein's theory of relativity, and that helped pay for the summer. By my junior year I decided that I had three possibilities for a major: history of science, philosophy of science, or mathematics. Physics was out of the question, since I had not yet taken any courses in physics. I did think that I should have at least one, so in my junior year I enrolled in freshman physics, taught by Wendell Furry.

Furry was certainly a lucid teacher. But, at least as I saw it, the whole thing lacked poetry. Furry was teaching to the convinced; this was real bread-and-butter classical physics, with hardly a mention of things like the theory of relativity or the quantum theory. Instead, there was a lot of experimental work, which I intensely disliked. This was also the era of the slide rule, and I found my myopia kept me from reading mine with ease. I did not, and do not, have the patience and manual dexterity for experimental physics.

That year, including the previous summer, I took six mathematics courses, three philosophy courses, and the course in physics, and by the end of the year had decided to major in mathematics. By this time, with all the extra courses I was taking, I had begun to catch up with some of my contemporaries who had *entered* Harvard with the idea of going into mathematics. I say "some" because I'd met a few of the really extraordinary mathematically gifted undergraduates that Harvard had attracted. The two who made the greatest impression on me were Marvin Minsky and Charles Zemach. Minsky, who a few years later became one of the creators of the discipline of artificial intelligence, was a little older than we were, because he had spent a couple of years in the navy. When I first knew him, he was garnering a distinctively erratic set of As and Ds in his courses, depending on how much they interested him. In his senior year he produced a brilliantly original thesis, which he never bothered to publish, and then went off to Princeton, where he started his work on the mathematics of artificial intelligence. Both he and Zemach, who is now at Los Alamos, had attended New York public schools. Minsky was a graduate of the Bronx High School of Science, and Zemach had attended Peter Stuyvesant High School. It is ironic to me that these two public schools, which my family would have regarded as dangerous places for me or any other child, had superb programs in science and mathematics that gave these budding geniuses everything they could absorb.

I will never forget my first meeting with Zemach. I had been looking for someone to play chess with, and a friend told me to try Zemach. I did, and we made a date to play one afternoon at his Harvard House. By coincidence I had spent the entire previous night solving the problem of the twelve balls, in which one is given twelve identical-looking balls and a balance scale. One of the balls is either lighter or heavier than the others. The problem is to find a method of making use of three, and only three, weighings to determine which is the "guilty" ball and whether it is lighter or heavier. It is not an easy problem, and it took me all night to solve it. In the afternoon, feeling triumphant, I went to play chess with Zemach. As we were setting up the chess pieces, I asked him whether he had ever heard of the problem of the twelve balls. He hadn't. But by the time he had finished setting up his pieces he had solved it. Not only that; he had begun to formulate an equation for determining how many weighings it would take to select the guilty ball from among n balls. I was astonished. It turned out that, although he was a junior, Zemach already had had almost the entire curriculum of the undergraduate courses in both physics and mathematics at Harvard and had, indeed, entered Harvard knowing most of the standard mathematics curriculum. He was completely unassuming about all of this — almost embarrassed — and lent me books that he thought might help me catch up. Even better, he told me about an informal seminar on the theory of relativity being given one evening a week by a young physicist named Bryce De Witt, now a professor at the University of Texas. I started going and for the first time began to understand Einstein's book.

My intention for my senior year was to learn enough mathematics so that I could go on and eventually do a Ph.D. thesis with George Mackey, who had long been interested in the relation of higher mathematics to physics. I also planned to take a few of the more mathematics-oriented graduate physics courses. As things turned out, I did the latter but never got to the former.

My senior year was a watershed in another sense. It was the last time I had any real contact with my high school world of jazz and show business. Duke Ellington's orchestra came to Boston. Of course I went to see it, and one night after a concert accompanied the Duke and some of my old friends from the orchestra to an Italian restaurant. Cat Anderson was no longer with the group, but I invited Al Sears to Sunday lunch at Eliot House. It seemed to me a natural thing to do. During all the years I had followed the jazz musicians, I had never given any thought to their being black and my being white. My father had always treated racism of all kinds with contempt, and had never thought twice about having Al Sears stay in our house in Rochester. It did not occur to me — and in this I was naïve — that Sears might feel uncomfortable in the all-white, preppy atmosphere of an Eliot House Sunday lunch. Sunday lunch was the meal to which students brought their parents or their girlfriends from Radcliffe, Wellesley, or Smith. I brought Sears. He was the only adult black person who was not waiting table or cleaning up. I sensed, and he certainly must have, that he was being studied as a kind of curiosity. We both felt acutely uncomfortable. To make matters worse, I was totally preoccupied with my senior mathematics thesis. Formulae were jumping around in my head, and I could hardly focus on our conversation. I had quite unconsciously become someone else; I was no longer the teenage boy following the bands. When Sears shook hands, rather sadly, and took his leave, it was the end of a part of my life. I never saw him again.

I graduated from Harvard in the spring of 1951. I had done well enough in my mathematics program so that I was admitted to the Harvard Graduate School as a graduate student in mathematics.

4

Deuteronomy

SOME TIME during the fall of 1953, when I was actually working on my doctoral thesis in theoretical physics, I ran into Chuck Zemach, who was engaged in a similar enterprise. My thesis concerned the electric and magnetic properties of the nucleus of heavy hydrogen — a neutron and proton stuck together, the so-called deuteron. I told Zemach that I planned to call my thesis "Deuteronomy." He said, with a wry smile, that he was planning to call his "Exodus." Indeed, each of us had a four-year plan that involved an exodus from Harvard with a Ph.D. in physics.

I had had a four-year plan from the day I entered graduate school, but it was not the one I ended up with. I had expected to get my doctorate in mathematics. The four-year time limit was mandated by finances. As an undergraduate, I had never qualified for a scholarship. My father's modest middle-class income was considered too high to put me in the category of real scholarship need; and with all my switching around of fields, my grades were not high enough, until the very end of my undergraduate days, for me to qualify for any of the few scholarships that were awarded independent of need. I did work in the summers, but my earnings barely paid for my summer school expenses. If I was to go to graduate school, I would have to pay my way, especially since my brother was about to go to college.

Short of stealing, there were two ways a graduate student could earn his or her way through graduate school at that time: with a fellowship or by teaching. The National Science Foundation had created a small number of fellowships for graduate study that were available on a competitive basis. I applied for one and got honorable mention, which was consoling but not edible. The other way — now for me the only way — was to get a teaching job. I heard that I. Bernard Cohen was looking for teaching assistants for Natural Sciences 3, the very course that had started everything off when I was a freshman. Fortunately, Cohen hired me. This was the genesis of my four-year plan. As I understood it, it was a policy of the graduate school to limit teaching fellowships to four years, though there were certainly exceptions. Tom Lehrer, with whom I was then taking mathematics courses, eventually spent eleven years in graduate school, ten at Harvard and one at Columbia, and taught for more than four years. But this was rare. I did not think I could or should count on such an exception and decided that, one way or another, I was going to get out in four years.

That settled, I needed a place to live. As it happened, Harvard had just built a spanking new graduate center, designed by Walter Gropius. I moved in. The design was perhaps slightly ahead of its time; it featured, along with cell-like rooms, a stainless steel statue by Richard Lippold that vaguely resembled a tree and was, in fact, named *World Tree*. In Einstein's theory of relativity the lines and curves plotted in four dimensions are called world lines, and that may have been what inspired Lippold. Anyway, the sculpture and the name led Tom Lehrer and a group of pranksters to organize two ceremonies in honor of the "tree." In the first, which coincided with the vernal equinox, some of the group dressed up as bulls, and a few unfortunates, dressed as "virgins," were sacrificed. Later that year there was an Arbor Day celebration at which "world seeds" (ball bearings) were planted under the tree and a metal "world bird" was put on a branch. I was discussing these matters at lunch one day in the graduate center with Lehrer, whom I had known from my undergraduate days, when a student waiter dropped an entire tray of dishes, making an unbelievable clatter. "They're playing our song," said Lehrer.

My principal activity that first year, apart from taking more graduate mathematics courses, was to learn quantum mechanics. I had been flirting with quantum mechanics all the way back in my freshman course with Professor Frank. I knew that it involved a much more radical departure from classical physics than did relativity, which is a fairly straightforward extension of the classical physics of Newton and Maxwell. The quantum theory is entirely new. I had read a number of popular and semipopular books on the quantum theory, and much of the mathematics I was studying had to do with it. When I first met him, George Mackey told me that he had been reading Hermann Weyl's *Group Theory and Quantum Mechanics* for some fifteen years, and that a large part of his own work had to do with making quantum mechanics mathematically rigorous. This was the program I thought I might like to work on, but I had never taken a really solid course in the quantum theory. It was at this point that I encountered the third great teacher of my Harvard days.

To the Harvard physics students of my generation, Julian Schwinger was a mythological figure. In order to reduce him to human proportions, we referred to him among ourselves by his first name: Julian had been spotted eating dinner with his wife at the Window Shop; Julian had been seen going to the Brattle Street Playhouse.

Julian Schwinger was born in New York City in 1918. A mathematics and physics prodigy, he taught himself most of the fundamentals by working through the technical articles in the *Encyclopaedia Britannica*. At the age of sixteen he wrote — but did not publish — his first technical paper in physics, which dealt with a problem in quantum electrodynamics. It is difficult to believe that his abilities would not have been recognized eventually, but as it happened he had the good fortune to have them discovered early by the American physicist I. I. Rabi, who was able to further Schwinger's career. "It was sort of romantic in a way," Rabi told me of his discovery of Schwinger. "You can fix it to a year, 1935." That was the year when Einstein, Boris Podolsky, and Nathan Rosen had published a celebrated paper showing just how different the quantum mechanical idea of reality was from that of classical physics. Echoes of this paper still reverberate.

I was reading the paper [Rabi went on], and my way of reading a paper was to bring in a student and explain it to him. In this case the student was Lloyd Motz, who's now a professor of astronomy at Columbia. We were arguing about something, and after a while Motz said there was someone waiting outside the office and asked if he could bring him in. He brought in this kid in knee pants. So I told him to sit down some place, and he sat down.

Motz and I were arguing, and this kid pipes up and settles the argument. And I said, "Who the hell is this?" Well, it turned out that he was a sophomore at City College, and he was doing very badly — flunking his courses, not in physics, but doing very badly. I talked to him for a while and was deeply impressed. He had already written a paper on quantum electrodynamics. I asked him if he wanted to transfer, and he said yes. Later he gave me a transcript, and I looked at it. He was failing English, and just about everything else, but he spoke well. I said, "What's the matter with you? You're flunking English. You speak well, and you sound like an educated person." He said, "I have no time for the themes." I tried to get him admitted to Columbia on a scholarship. The director of admissions looked at the transcript and said, "A scholarship?" He wouldn't even admit him.

Rabi is not one to be easily put off. He had a couple of prominent theoretical physicists, Hans Bethe and George Uhlenbeck, read Schwinger's paper and plead his cause. It worked. Rabi claims that Schwinger turned over a new leaf; indeed, he did make Phi Beta Kappa. But something of the old Schwinger remained. He registered for a course with Uhlenbeck and almost never showed up in class. Nor did he do the homework, and there was a question as to whether he was going to take the final. Uhlenbeck was a visiting professor at Columbia, and Rabi got a hold of Schwinger and told him that he was not being considerate to a visitor. Schwinger took the final. Not only did he get a perfect grade; he also did the problems by using Uhlenbeck's own mathematical notation, which he must have discovered by looking at someone else's notes before the exam.

By the time Schwinger graduated from Columbia College he had already done all the work necessary for his Ph.D. thesis. But Columbia had a two-year graduate student residence requirement, so Schwinger stayed on for two years, during which time he worked as the theorist in Rabi's laboratory. After Schwinger received his Ph.D., Rabi placed him with his old friend and colleague Robert Oppenheimer in California, where he remained until the war. When the war broke out Rabi and Schwinger both went to the Radiation Laboratory in Cambridge, where radar was being developed. According to Rabi, Schwinger worked all night at the Radiation Laboratory and slept all day. "At five o'clock when everybody was leaving, you'd see Schwinger coming in." People who had left mathematical problems on their desks or on blackboards would often find them solved anonymously the next morning. Rabi recalled, "The problems he solved were just fantastic. He lectured twice a week on his current work." Following the lectures, the more experimentally inclined physicists in the audience would use Schwinger's ideas to invent new radars. In 1946 Schwinger was appointed an associate professor in physics at Harvard and a year later, at twenty-nine, he became one of the youngest full professors in the history of the university.

Schwinger gave courses in all branches of theoretical physics. Like Mackey's, these courses were completely original. It was a standing joke in the profession at the time that almost any unsolved problem in theoretical physics could be found solved in Schwinger's unpublished classroom notes. As it happened — and this was a piece of luck — when I entered graduate school, in the fall of 1951, Schwinger was starting a cycle of quantum mechanics lectures that, in the end, would last for a year and a half. These lectures were a kind of theater. Like any great performer, Schwinger would always be slightly late.

Since he still worked all night, the classes were scheduled for the late morning. He drove a small blue Cadillac — the make of car also set him apart from the herd — and a scout would watch out for its arrival, at which point we would all rush into the classroom to find seats. In those days Schwinger was averse to most forms of physical exercise. When I got to know him better, he would occasionally kid me about my tennis playing and bicycle riding. Later, after he left Harvard and went to the University of California at Los Angeles, Schwinger became, I am told, an avid tennis player. But at the time I speak of he had a slightly oblate look, accentuated by the stark white pallor of his skin, the result of his nocturnal hours. There was a remarkable Indian graduate student in the class who said to me one day, apropos of nothing evident, "*Our* Schwinger is very fat." By the standards of rural India, he certainly was.

To add to the general sense of theater, Schwinger never used, at least in those days, any lecture notes. As one who has spent much of the last thirty years giving lectures in theoretical physics, I find this nearly incomprehensible. He did incredibly complicated calculations on the blackboard without the shred of a note. This goes beyond memorization, although that may have played a part. The individual steps of these calculations were, one gathers, so trivial to Schwinger that he could carry them out more or less spontaneously. However, he did not like to be interrupted, and questions in class were not encouraged. You had the feeling that you were assisting in a remarkable performance, and just as you would not stand up in a theater and ask a question of an actor while he was working, so you did not ask questions of Schwinger. Schwinger also had some speech mannerisms that many of his students began unconsciously to imitate. By

1975, when Schwinger left Harvard, he had produced sixty-eight Ph.D.s, an incredibly high number for a theorist when you consider that each Ph.D. represents at least one publishable research idea. I don't know how many of these acolytes began to say "nucular" and "we can effectively regard," two of the Schwinger locutions. One of my contemporaries constructed what I thought was the perfect model of a Schwinger sentence. It began "Although 'one' is not perfectly 'zero,' we can effectively regard . . ." In short, Julian was another legend.

My own position in this course was rather anomalous. Quantum mechanics was a reaction to the inadequacies of classical physics when applied on the atomic scale. But I knew no classical physics, other than parts of the theory of relativity. For example, I had never had — and as things worked out, never would have — a course in classical electrodynamics, to say nothing of statistical mechanics. I also had not had a conventional course in quantum theory, so I could not fully appreciate the originality of what Schwinger was doing. (Many of the methods he introduced in these lectures later found their way into general use in the physics community, but it took years for that to happen.) Nonetheless, I was fascinated by what I did manage to understand. As a consequence, I decided to take the graduate-level course in *classical* mechanics, which was nominally the prerequisite for Schwinger's course. Hence, in my second year as a graduate student I took the continuation of Schwinger's course along with its prerequisite. At some point during the semester rumblings in the mathematics department began to be heard, and these, as it happened, coincided with my own feeling about my future in pure mathematics.

To someone with little knowledge of higher mathematics, it is hard to explain the distinction between being able to create pure mathematics and being able to understand it. Such a lay person will assume that if you do well in a large number of courses in higher mathematics, you must be a mathematician. Perhaps I can illustrate the point by describing something that happened to me at about this time. I was taking a graduate course in the theory of complex variables and doing perfectly well in it. One Sunday evening I went to the graduate center's communal shower and — those being relatively innocent days — didn't lock the door to my cubicle. When I returned, I was startled to discover a small bright-eyed Indian sitting cross-legged in the middle of my bed. He looked rather like something you would conjure up by rubbing a lamp. He said that he, too, was taking the complex variables course, but that he never went to class and would therefore like to glance through my notes.

Later, when I got to know him, he told me why he didn't go to class. When he first came from India to Boston he had been involved in an ugly racial incident. It was so traumatic that he had decided not to go out again during daylight hours. He slept or kept to himself during the day and came out at night like a nocturnal animal. We got into the habit of discussing the course and anything else that came to mind, and we became quite good friends. Listening to him talk about the course, I understood just what it meant to be a real mathematician. My friend moved among abstract ideas as if they were the familiar flowers in a garden. He saw the concepts as vividly and effortlessly as if they were living things. He knew instinctively what statements were true long before he came to proving anything. The proofs, which he could supply if asked, were secondary to the truth.

I, on the other hand, had to proceed systematically and usually without that kind of sure-handed intuition. Given this, I didn't see how I was going to be able to create anything in mathematics, or where the new ideas would come from. And I didn't see any purpose in becoming a mathematician if I couldn't create the stuff. Although I knew very little about physics, it seemed to me that I could do useful work simply by working at it. I would never become a Schwinger, but I might become a useful physicist. I also realized that the more abstract the mathematics became, the less interesting I found it. If it did not have some application to reality, it seemed to me to be a sort of game. This may have been a corollary to my feeling that I could not create it, or it may reflect a basic distinction between having the temperament for pure mathematics and not having it. In any event, that was my dilemma.

I once heard a story about a monk who left the Benedictine order. When asked why, he gave seven reasons, the last of which was "They kicked me out." The mathematics department certainly did not kick me out, but its chairman, Garrett Birkhoff, told me that I would have to choose, now that I was about to get my master's degree, between physics and mathematics. I could not go on in the mathematics department while taking most of my course work in physics. At this point I decided to talk to the chairman of the physics department, an experimental physicist named J. Curry Street. I was not at all sure the physics department would have me, considering my bizarre list of courses, which, apart from anything else, did not include a single course in experimental physics. In retrospect I am not entirely sure why the physics department did agree to admit me. I suppose it had relatively little to lose, since I was paying my way by working as an instructor for Cohen in Natural Sciences 3. However, it did impose some conditions. I was to spend a summer working as an assistant at the Harvard Cyclotron, learning something about experimental nuclear physics, and the following fall I was to take an oral examination in experimental nuclear physics. With a good many misgivings, I agreed.

It was now the spring of 1953, a lovely spring, as I recall, marred only by Cohen's firing me as an instructor in his course. In a sense this was not entirely unexpected. The same course that had enchanted me as a freshman was being taught by Cohen in the same way, with the same phrases, and the same round handwriting on the blackboard. But now it all seemed a little trivial. The students apparently felt this too. The "Confi Guide" of 1955 reported:

> Many polls chided Master of Ceremonies I. B. Cohen for his pompous style of delivery. Inveterate name dropper . . . Cohen was frequently accused of beating around the bush, and then making a point without . . . an adequate progressing explanation. He was praised by all for his remarkable organization, particularly at the beginning of the year. His book, which bears the same title as the course (*The Nature and Growth of the Physical Sciences*), was found . . . to contain largely the same material as the lectures and hence attendance could be readily substituted for by reading — and vice versa.

It is very hard to fool undergraduates.

I find it impossible to conceal how I feel about things, especially if I don't like them, so I imagine my attitude toward Cohen and the course must have been fairly transparent. To add to it all, Cohen had just engaged a young instructor, who had recently left the navy, to oversee the rest of us and the administrative details of a course that involved nearly four hundred students. This fellow had several brainstorms, including obligatory attendance by the instructors at lectures and a new way of keeping grades. All the grades were kept in the "Big Book," and each of us was to keep a "Little Book" with our own grades. This doubled my bookkeeping chores, and all that really mattered, I felt, was what was in the "Big Book." It was a small point, but I had a lot on my mind, and I didn't feel like keeping an extra set of grades for almost a hundred students. I was scrupulous about putting the grades in the "Big Book," but my "Little Book" was blank. How this came to Cohen's attention I do not know, but late that spring we had an instructors' meeting at which Cohen asked to see my "Little Book." It happened to be safely residing in my room in the graduate center, and I was sent to fetch it. The day was lovely, and I recall sitting under a flowering tree, desultorily putting some grades into my "Little Book." I finally got up from my tree and returned to the meeting. After looking at my book, Cohen announced stentoriously that I would not be continuing with the course the next semester.

This was a potential disaster, not only for my four-year plan but for my whole program of graduate study. And then I had one of those strokes of fortune that can decide a person's future. During my undergraduate years I had gotten to know Gerald Holton reasonably well. Like me, he was a disciple of Philipp Frank, whom we privately referred to as Uncle Philipp. Holton had taken his doctorate with Percy Bridgman and was now doing experimental work on the physics of high pressures. But he was also a historian of science with interest in the philosophy of science. He was, in some sense, a model of what I thought I would like to be. Furthermore, he was sharing the teaching responsibilities in Natural Science 2, a more serious version of the course that Cohen was teaching. It attracted people who were not science majors but who had some scientific orientation. The course was run by Edwin C. Kemble, a theoretical physicist who was one of the first American physicists to become trained, in the 1920s, in the then new quantum physics. I always thought of Mr. Kemble as "old Mr. Kemble"; although in 1953 he was just sixty-four, he seemed ancient. (He died in 1984 at the age of ninety-five.) Kemble was slow of speech, had a gravelly voice, and looked like a New England sea captain. He did not do things lightly or hastily. When Holton told me that Kemble was looking for a new section man, I went at once to see him.

Professor Kemble had heard of my contretemps with Cohen and had decided that I might be some kind of flake. After our interview he even questioned my fellow graduate students to see whether they considered me a serious person. The reports were apparently favorable, and I was hired provisionally, with the understanding that if I did not take my responsibilities dutifully, I would be let go. Fair enough.

That now left me with a summer at the Harvard Cyclotron. Located in a brick building not far from the campus, the Harvard Cyclotron was the first particle accelerator I ever saw. As these machines go, it was relatively small, having been completed early, in 1948. I knew nothing about how such machines are run, so I was in no position to realize just how simple the operation of this one was. Run mainly by graduate students and a few postdoctoral fellows and junior faculty, it was an ideal teaching tool, because the graduate students could get their hands on everything. The big machines now have entire corps of engineers who actually run them while the physicists confine themselves to planning experiments and analyzing the data that are taken by computers. There are even specialists who design the detectors and the targets. At the cyclotron we did everything — in fact, we did so much of everything that I had no time to understand what it was that we were doing.

I was attached to a small group directed by Walter Selove, then a junior faculty member at Harvard and now a professor at the University of Pennsylvania. We were an odd collection. One of my colleagues was Paul Fenimore Cooper, Jr., a descendent of the novelist. Paul, known as Nicky, had had a combined major in both classics and physics, and was doing graduate work with Selove. There was also a rough-hewn Texan whose name I cannot remember. Nicky, as befitting a classicist, had an elegant turn of phrase. Late one night we were piling lead bricks, which were used for shielding, and Nicky dropped one on his foot. He emitted a stream of profanity which so shocked the Texan that he stopped what he was doing and, pointing to Nicky, said, in utter disbelief, "Look, he's cussin'!"

We piled bricks and sometimes actually sewed together by hand the pieces of material that were to be used for targets. The cyclotron circulated at moderate energies protons that impinged on the targets we sewed. Some years later I finally understood the point of what we were doing: the protons were allowed to pick up a neutron on passing through a nucleus, thereby forming my beloved deuteron. The process was known as deuteron pickup. To me it was piling lead bricks and sewing targets. Whatever it was, the summer passed without incident and without my learning much about experimental nuclear physics, the subject of my forthcoming oral examination.

The year 1953–1954 was for me a very complicated one. I was still determined to finish my degree in not more than four years. Since I had already spent two, that left two, and the time had come for me to begin working on my thesis. The most obvious thing, I suppose, would have been to try to work with Schwinger. But every Wednesday there was a line of graduate students outside his office, hoping to get a few minutes of his time. I did not see how, given my background, I was going to be able to work on a thesis problem with that little help — assuming that Schwinger would even take me on. There were, however, some junior faculty members who did not have many students, were closer to me in age than was Schwinger, and seemed willing to have new students. Among them was Abraham Klein, a Harvard Junior Fellow. Like Selove, he is now a professor at the University of Pennsylvania. Klein was very energetic and full of ideas for calculations, so I signed up to do a thesis with him. I have no idea whether he had any idea that he was taking on someone who knew next to nothing about physics. He did, however, have a straightforward-sounding problem involving the electromagnetic properties of the deuteron. This was a time when there were several competing models of the nuclear force, each of which could be tested by being tried out on the deuteron. Klein was interested in one of the models, and he proposed that we try it on the deuteron's electromagnetic properties. Thus I was launched on a thesis.

Meanwhile there was the oral examination and the course requirement to worry about. First the oral, which I took late that fall. That can be discussed simply. I failed it. My failure was of a very particular kind. I was asked a number of questions that anyone with a modest grasp of physics would have answered with no difficulty. I answered the questions in a very roundabout mathematical way, provoking much mirth among the examiners. A less flexible institution might have flunked me out, and that would have been that. Instead, I was told that if I took a course in experimental physics the following spring and passed it, I would satisfy the requirement. I agreed. At the same time, Kenneth Bainbridge — a gentle and kind experimental physicist who had played a key role at Los Alamos during the war, and who had become the chairman of the department — suggested that I take a reading course with Wendell Furry in the theory of electromagnetic radiation. He told me that Furry had been one of Oppenheimer's students and that I could learn a great deal from him. So I signed up with Furry, who had taught the freshman physics course I took when I was a junior.

I think it is important to the sequel for me to describe Wendell Furry. He was a solid-looking man with a large stomach that spilled over his pants. He looked and talked like a small-town Midwesterner who might own a garage. He seemed to cultivate his image of being something of an eccentric, a bit of a bumpkin. He was, however, especially in the 1930s, a superb theoretical physicist. Even now I keep learning about contributions Furry made, especially to the quantum theory of radiation. He seemed the most apolitical person imaginable. Both during the course I took with him as a junior and during the reading course, when I was with him alone for many hours, there was never the remotest hint that he had any interest in politics or, indeed, in anything very worldly. It came as a shock that Furry had been a member of the Communist Party for some years after 1938, and that even as I was taking his course, he and the university were under siege by Joseph McCarthy.

One of the strangest documents I have saved from those years is a reprint of the stenographic transcript of the hearings of the Permanent Subcommittee on Investigations of the Committee on Government Operations of the United States Senate, Boston, Massachusetts, January 15, 1954. What is especially odd about the copy I have is that it is signed by the principal participants. Furry wrote, "Best regards, W. H. Furry"; Leon J. Kamin, the other witness, wrote, simply, in a careful script, "Leon J. Kamin"; and McCarthy signed with a bold flourish, in very large letters, "Joseph R. McCarthy." I have no recollection of asking for the autographs, yet there they are. It seems very peculiar that McCarthy would have signed so flamboyantly, just beneath the signatures of the two men he had pilloried. But he did.

This was Furry's second appearance before the committee. He had appeared on November 4, 1953, and had refused, on constitutional grounds, to answer any questions at all. Meanwhile, the university had taken a position that sounded morally acceptable but that put witnesses like Furry in serious legal jeopardy. The university maintained that if they wanted to retain their jobs, faculty members called to testify would have to reveal their own activities but would not have to "name names" — reveal the identities of their associates. This placed a man like Furry, for example, in danger of being cited for contempt, since in agreeing to answer some questions about his Communist past, he had in effect given up his immunity. McCarthy, of course, understood the situation and exploited it for all it was worth. Furry began the hearings by making a statement:

Our forefathers wrote into the Constitution the privilege of the Fifth Amendment to provide protection which good citizens may sometimes sorely need. Innocent people who feel the threat of false, mistaken, or overzealous prosecution because of unpopular opinions have every right to invoke this protection. It is clear, however, that widespread misrepresentation has produced in many minds a distorted idea of the meaning of the constitutional privilege. Though its real purpose has always been to shield the innocent, many people have been misled into believing that the exercise of the privilege is an admission of guilt. I have now come to the belief that for me to continue to claim my constitutional privilege would bring undue harm to me and to the great institution with which I am connected.

Although I am sure that my past claims to the privilege have been both legally justified and morally right, I now intend to waive my constitutional rights and give this committee all the evidence it may legitimately seek concerning my own activities and associations. I hope that by telling my own political history I can help to dispel suspicion and contribute to public understanding.

Experience has taught me that the inquiry is likely to concern other persons than myself. I feel obliged to state now that I shall respectfully refuse to answer questions that bring in the names of other people. I wish to make it clear, however, that if I knew of any person whose conduct as I saw it was criminal, I should feel bound to reveal the facts. I am not seeking to protect the guilty from prosecution. I wish merely to shield the innocent from persecution. I hope that on this matter the committee will respect my conscience.

In his response McCarthy showed what he thought of Furry's conscience. "May I say, Mr. Furry," he said, "that a man who has been a member of the Communist conspiracy is not exactly the last word on who is guilty and who is innocent." Furry claimed, and I have every reason to believe him, that he had not been a member of the Communist Party for many years when this confrontation took place. In fact, from his testimony, one got the impression that Furry was thoroughly disillusioned with Communism by this time. McCarthy, however, stated, "It is not up to you to decide that; it is not up to us to decide that. It is up to this committee to expose the facts. It is up to the law-enforcing agencies to decide who should be prosecuted."

There then followed a kind of deadly cat-and-mouse game, in which McCarthy tried again and again to trick or coerce Furry into naming names. At one point the dialogue resembled an Ionesco play. Furry admitted that there had been about "half a dozen" members of the Communist Party working with him on radar during the war. He added, "By my observation they were among the more security-minded members of this laboratory. They never in any way departed from the rules, to my knowledge, or showed any inclination to regard any outside connections, including that with the Communist Party, as having any bearing on their work. They were devoted to the war effort, they worked loyally, and I shall not reveal their names." McCarthy decided that Furry might talk if he gave the six men numbers instead of names. "Let's take them by number instead of name," he said, overlooking the probability that his numbers and Furry's numbers might be entirely different. The dialogue went as follows:

> THE CHAIRMAN: Let's take Number 2. When did you last see Number 2?
> MR. FURRY: Of course, I have to decide who is Number 2.

THE CHAIRMAN: You pick out Number 2.

MR. FURRY: And there are a number of these people that I have really very little notion when I last saw them. It has been some time within the last few years.

THE CHAIRMAN: You said there were six. You were a Communist and they were Communists. You say you will not give the name. I am trying to identify them by number. Let's take Number 2. When did you last see him?

MR. FURRY: Well, for Number 2, I will take a man of whom I am not sure just when I last saw him, but it was within the last year or two, and I know from professional connections just where he is working.

THE CHAIRMAN: Where is he working?

MR. FURRY: In an American university and I am pretty sure on nothing connected with government work, certainly no secret work.

THE CHAIRMAN: Is he teaching?

MR. FURRY: Yes. It is my impression that his work is just like mine at the present, teaching and research of what you might call the free-enterprise kind, which still exists in this country.

THE CHAIRMAN: What is his name?

MR. FURRY: I refuse to state.

THE CHAIRMAN: You are ordered to state it.

MR. FURRY: I refuse.

THE CHAIRMAN: Number 3 . . .

And so on, through the whole list.

After some more parrying, McCarthy turned his attention to the university. He asked, "Do you know of anyone connected with Harvard who is or was a member of the Communist Party?" To which Furry replied, "Sir, I am not sorting people for the committee."

THE CHAIRMAN: Answer the question.

MR. FURRY: Well, I would like to make this statement, and that is that I have never at any time known anyone who held a permanent position on the Harvard faculty, with the exception of myself, or who has since come to hold or who now holds a permanent position on the Harvard faculty, to be a member of the Communist Party. Apart from that, I will refuse to answer the question.

Finally McCarthy erupted in rage.

This, in the opinion of the chair, is one of the most aggravated cases of contempt that we have had before us, as I see it. Here you have a man teaching at one of our large universities. He knows there were six Communists handling secret government work, radar work, atomic work. He refuses to give either the committee or the FBI or anyone else the information which he has. To me it is inconceivable that a university which has had the reputation of being a great university would keep this type of creature on teaching our children. Because of men like this who have refused to give the government the information which they have in their own minds about Communists who are working on our secret work, many young men have died in the past, and if we lose a war in the future it will be the result of the lack of loyalty, complete (immorality) [unmorality] of these individuals who continue to protect the conspirators.

With that, the hearing ended. On her way out of the hearing room, one Boston woman spat on Furry.

I never got to know Furry well enough to know how deeply, and in what ways, all of this affected him, but he certainly struck me as a beaten man. His situation was not made happier, I am sure, by the brilliance of Schwinger, so much younger and so talented. I have a vivid memory of sitting in one of Schwinger's lectures, a year or so later, and seeing Furry in the middle of the classroom,

auditing. What was strange was that he was ostenta-
tiously turning over the pages of *Time* magazine during
the lecture. If Schwinger noticed, he did not let on. During my reading course with Furry, which preceded these
public hearings but coincided with his first appearance
before the committee, I was completely unaware of Furry's personal ordeal. It is true that Furry was away from
time to time in Washington, but many people in the
physics department went to Washington. At the end of
the semester I produced a term paper on the electron,
which I still have. It came back with a single comment
in red pencil by Furry on a minor matter of notation. This
was a few weeks before his public hearing, and I wonder
whether he had had time to read the whole thing.

Furry was indicted for contempt of Congress, but the
case was eventually dismissed by Judge Bailey Aldrich. I
am not sure why, except that Harvard, with all its well-
placed alumni and all of its faculty engaged in vital government service, was a rather formidable opponent.
McCarthy did not do well when he went after powerful
targets like the army. He died in 1957. Furry remained at
Harvard and was for a while the chairman of the department. He retired in 1977, and died in 1984. I wonder
whether the students who came in contact with him in
later years had any notion of what he had gone through
that fall and winter.

Not long after Furry's hearing I had my first close-up view
of Robert Oppenheimer. The incident, which does require
a little explanation, taught me a basic lesson about the
press. My father had a long and close relationship with
the theoretical physicist Robert Marshak, former president of the City College of New York. Marshak had been
at Los Alamos during the war, and after the war he

returned to Rochester and became chairman of the physics department at the university. He married a Rochester woman, Ruth Gupp, who had been one of my Sunday school teachers. When I began to study things like relativity and the quantum theory, I had some talks with Marshak, and he even gave me a tour of the university's experimental facilities. Marshak had great ambitions to put the University of Rochester on the map in physics, and he certainly did help to make the department first-rate. One of the things he did was to create what became known as the Rochester Conferences. These were meetings, lasting several days, that brought together the best people from all over the world in high-energy and elementary-particle physics. Invitations to the conferences were highly prized and hard to come by. It was unthinkable for a graduate student like me to have an invitation to a Rochester Conference.

The conference was usually timed to coincide with a university vacation period so that the facilities in Rochester would be available and university professors would be free to come. In 1954 the conference was held in late January, the time of my winter break from school, so, *par force des choses*, I was in Rochester at my parents' house.

Marshak did a very kind thing. He said I could come to the conference as a student, with the understanding that I would sit with the University of Rochester graduate students in the balcony and keep my mouth shut. The next morning, bright and early, I appeared on campus and found my way to the building where the meeting was being held. Before I could find my way to the balcony I was grabbed by a reporter from the Rochester *Times Union*, the local evening paper, and asked whether I was a conference participant. I said no, I was a graduate student in physics and was a guest, along with the other graduate students. What I should have done was run like hell. The reporter said it was fine that I was a student, since he was interviewing people at all levels. He took me to a room and asked some questions while the flash bulbs went off. I was a bit dazed but spent the day happily attending the meeting. That evening the paper was delivered to our house. On page fifteen there was a large headline: Physics — A Young Man's Game. Underneath, several inches down the page, was an even larger headline: It's Kids Who Hit Jackpot, Declares "Graybeard" of 49. The graybeard was Robert Oppenheimer, staring reverently upward from a small picture toward three large pictures at the top of the page. To the right was Geoffrey Chew, then of the University of Illinois and now at Berkeley, who was one of the stars of that Rochester Conference. To his right was a picture of Yoichiro Nambu, one of the most imaginative theoretical physicists of the postwar period, now at the University of Chicago, and to his right was I, looking vaguely like a young Woody Allen. The text was even worse. The part referring to us began, "The young physicists Oppenheimer admires have come to the conference from different levels of nuclear work. Jeremy Bernstein, a Rochestarian, is a graduate student in Harvard's physics department. He's 24." Needless to say, Oppenheimer did not know me from Mary Poppins, and I had never met Nambu and Chew, whom Oppenheimer really *did* admire. And needless to say, the publication of this article put an end to my appearance at the Rochester Conference of 1954.

I returned to Cambridge and continued to work on my thesis, take courses, and teach. In the spring I man-

aged to pass the experimental physics course, partly, perhaps, because the professor, R. V. Pound, derived a sort of
wry amusement from watching me fumble around with
the apparatus. I recall one afternoon when he spent about
an hour trying to extract a screw from some machinery
into which I had managed to drop it. He must have understood that I had no vocation for experimental physics and
was just trying to survive his course. The other bit of luck
was my lab partner, Paul Condon, the son of the noted
physicist E. U. Condon and the brother of Joseph Condon,
now an instrumental physicist at the AT&T Bell Labs.
Paul, like Joe, was a gifted experimental physicist. We
evolved a *modus operandi* according to which I was not
to touch anything but could offer commentary. At the end
of the semester each of us was to give a talk on a subject
in physics that interested us. I chose, with much malice
aforethought, an obscure aspect of the quantum theory of
fields and got a good deal of satisfaction from watching
Pound nod off to sleep as I droned on and on.

The teaching, on the other hand, was really satisfy-
ing. As it happened, I got to do most of the section work
for Natural Sciences 2 and even gave a few of the classroom lectures. I liked and respected both Holton and
Kemble and was determined to erase whatever negatives
there were in my reputation as a responsible teacher. The
"Confi Guide" remarked in its evaluation that I "added a
bit of whimsy to the course." I never quite knew what
that meant but decided to take it as a compliment.

My thesis work with Klein consisted of two
stages — three, if one counts the initial stage of understanding what the problem was. The problem was reasonably clear. The model of the deuteron being used at that
time was a neutron and proton held together by the ex-

change of lighter mesons called pi mesons. These days, it is more useful for some purposes to think of the deuteron as a kind of bag containing six quarks. The pi mesons are electrically charged, and therefore they set up additional electric currents in the deuteron. They are known as exchange currents, because they arise from the exchange of these mesons between the neutron and proton. There were, at the time I speak of, several different versions of the meson theory of nuclear forces, each one entailing somewhat different exchange currents in the deuteron. It was perfectly reasonable, therefore, to pick one of these models and compute the exchange currents. That was, in essence, the problem. Klein was one of the acknowledged experts in a meson model that bore the names of Tamm and Dancoff, after its progenitors. He taught me, with great patience, what I needed to know about this model to begin calculating, and he was sufficiently interested in the results to do many of the calculations in parallel as a check. Doing these calculations was the second stage, and with Klein's help it went fairly rapidly.

Then came the third stage. What we had derived were rather complicated mathematical formulae, and what we wanted were numbers. This was in 1954, just before the era in which electronic scientific computation became commonplace. At MIT a new computer, the Whirlwind, was being installed; indeed, a year or so later a friend of mine who had done a similar thesis at Cal Tech was able to get his expressions evaluated on that computer in a few hours. Programmable pocket calculators of the kind that now sell in drugstores for about forty dollars were a thing of the future. With one of those I very likely could have done my problem in a week. But what I had was a Marchant electromechanical arithmetic calculator, which worked by a series of motors and gears. By taking a number and dividing it by zero — the result being infinity — you could make the machine continue to calculate until smoke came out of it. It was incredibly slow by modern standards, and it ultimately took me about six months to do the computations, though it's true that I could not work at them full time because of the other things I was doing. Still, the beauty of my thesis problem was that it was a sure thing. I knew that if I kept at it, there would be an answer, and I could predict with certainty that I would get out the following year and thereby fulfill my four-year plan.

Understanding now how these things work, I can see that my expecting to finish by June 1955 must have been known in the department, because in the spring of 1954 I got two job nibbles. The first was a letter from a border state university of no special distinction asking whether I would be interested in being considered for the job of instructor after I got my degree. The writer went on to say that my name had been given to his department by the chairman of the Harvard physics department. I had an instinctive feeling that going to an out-of-the-way institution would be a disaster for me. Einstein once said that he would have liked to be a lighthouse attendant, because the job would have left him plenty of time to continue his research. Einstein very likely could have continued his research in a lighthouse, but for most of us such a placement would be a sure way to end a career. This place was not a lighthouse, but it was sufficiently isolated intellectually that I saw no future in it. Some months later, at a meeting, I ran into the man who had written me the letter. When I thanked him for having made the offer he remarked, casually, that it was lucky I hadn't accepted it;

the place was so bad that he had since taken another job.

The second nibble was even more strange. On the Harvard junior physics faculty was a brilliant young theorist, of Austrian descent, named Robert Karplus. He and Abraham Klein had collaborated on an important paper exploiting some of Schwinger's ideas. As was customary with those holding such junior appointments, Karplus was given a sabbatical leave, which he took at the University of California at Berkeley. About a year earlier, the Livermore Laboratory, under the influence of Edward Teller, had been set up in the hills near Berkeley as a kind of counterweight to Los Alamos. Teller felt that the Los Alamos scientists were not working with sufficient enthusiasm on the crash program to build the hydrogen bomb that President Truman had announced in January 1950. Karplus had been a consultant at Livermore, and when he returned to Harvard in the winter of 1954, he told me that he had given my name to Edward Teller as someone who might be recruited to Livermore. At the time, I did not have any moral feelings against going to a place like Livermore or Los Alamos. For whatever reasons, they were not regarded by my fellow students as very prestigious places to work in, but that had to do with the intellectual quality, as we perceived it, of the work and not with moral reservations about nuclear weapons. That came, for people of my generation, later.

In April of 1954 the American Physical Society, our professional organization, held its annual meeting in Washington. Graduate students were encouraged to go to APS meetings to learn what was going on and to get a sense of the job market. Now that I was a "physicist," I decided to go, and Karplus said that he would make an appointment for me to see Teller. The 1954 meeting was held in a large Washington hotel, and on one of the floors there was what we called the slave market — tables and booths at which prospective employers could meet possible future physicist employees. I no longer remember how I arranged to find Teller, but what happened next I will never forget.

He had a suite in which he was interviewing people, and he invited me up to it. There he told me that on the following day he was scheduled to give a talk on meson physics, and that the way he prepared talks was to give them first spontaneously with someone listening. He proposed to give his talk with me as the audience. I was to interrupt if I heard something wrong. Teller proceeded to pace up and down the room reciting his talk, of which I understood next to nothing. It was on a slightly eccentric meson theory that has long since disappeared. Since I understood almost nothing, I said nothing. At one point he stopped and said what a relief it was to be talking about physics rather than politics, a cryptic remark that I also did not understand. After the talk he said goodbye, and I left the room. I never heard from him or from Livermore. However, I soon learned the meaning of his remark.

A few days earlier — on April 28, 1954 — Teller had appeared as a witness "in the matter of J. Robert Oppenheimer," the security-clearance hearings that destroyed Oppenheimer's public career. Teller was a hostile witness, and many physicists, myself among them, have never been able to forgive him for what he said and the way that he said it. One of the charges that had been levelled against Oppenheimer was a lack of enthusiasm for building the hydrogen bomb. Among the points the hearing committee — a special panel of the Atomic Energy Committee —

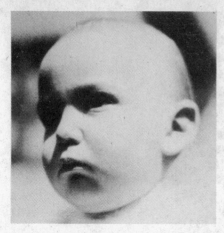

When I look at pictures of myself as a young child it seems to me that the little boy staring out of the pictures could be anyone.

In 1938 the four of us took a trip to Europe and the Middle East. My mother, Stephen, and I remained in England while my father went to Germany, where he saw for himself what was taking place in that wretched country.

The caption under my Columbia Grammar senior yearbook picture is "Young Man with a Horn."

Once the war was over, my parents returned to Rochester. I thought I would go back, too, but as it turned out I never did, at least not to live.

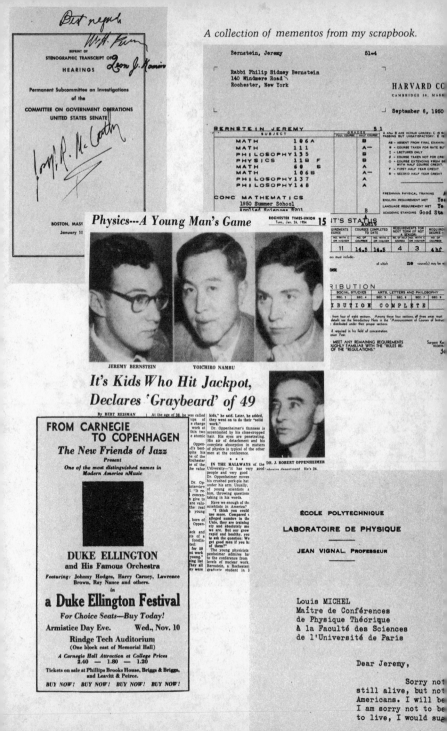

A collection of mementos from my scrapbook.

Bernstein, Jeremy   51-4

Rabbi Philip Sidney Bernstein
140 Windmere Road
Rochester, New York

HARVARD CO
CAMBRIDGE 38, MASS

September 6, 1950

BERNSTEIN JEREMY   51
SUBJECT

MATH	106A		B
MATH	111		A—
PHILOSOPHY	135		B
PHYSICS	118	F	B
MATH	60	S	A—
MATH	106B		A—
PHILOSOPHY	137		A
PHILOSOPHY	148		A

CONC MATHEMATICS
1950 Summer School

Physics---A Young Man's Game

ROCHESTER TIMES-UNION Tues., Jan. 26, 1954   15

JEREMY BERNSTEIN   YOICHIRO NAMBU

*It's Kids Who Hit Jackpot,
Declares 'Graybeard' of 49*

By BERT REISMAN

DR. J. ROBERT OPPENHEIMER

ÉCOLE POLYTECHNIQUE

LABORATOIRE DE PHYSIQUE

JEAN VIGNAL, PROFESSEUR

Louis MICHEL
Maître de Conférences
de Physique Théorique
à la Faculté des Sciences
de l'Université de Paris

Dear Jeremy,

Sorry not
still alive, but not
Americans. I will be
I am sorry not to be
to live, I would sug

— Maison des Etats-

When I entered Harvard, I. B. Cohen's Natural Sciences 3 was the lowest possible level science course and so I enrolled. There was something pleasantly reassuring about the way he wrote the formulae; they had round, nonthreatening shapes. The classroom demonstrations were entertaining and equally nonthreatening.

Wendell Furry looked and talked like a small-town Midwesterner who might own a garage. I found his classical physics course lacking poetry, but he was an exceptional theoretical physicist.

A mathematics and physics prodigy, Julian Schwinger would work at night and sleep during the day. At the Radiation Laboratory in Cambridge, where he worked during the war, people would arrive in the morning to find problems they had left on their desks or blackboards the night before anonymously solved.

I spent the summer of 1957 at Los Alamos, New Mexico, where I began a lifelong friendship with Francis Low, with whom I played innumerable games of tennis and with whom I traveled to Nevada one weekend to watch an atomic bomb test at sunrise. Francis is shown here on the right with Kenneth Johnson at the Center for Theoretical Physics at MIT.

When I collapsed on the sixth page of The Meaning of Relativity and realized it was not going to be like reading Scott's Lady of the Lake after all, I enrolled in Philipp Frank's Physics 16, which focused on philosophical and historical questions concerning modern science, most particularly the theory of relativity.

When I finished my graduate studies there was one place in all
the world that I wanted to go, and that was the Institute for
Advanced Study at Princeton. Although Einstein had died in
1955, I still thought of the Institute as his.

When I first met Oppenheimer and explained I would be coming to the Institute,
his face lit up like a sunrise and he reeled
off a list of who would be there that fall. It
sounded like a guest list for a Nobel Prize
banquet. That first conversation with him
gave me a glimpse of what he described in
a letter to his young brother Frank as "physics and the obvious excellences of the life it
brings."

I soon got my first view of Freeman Dyson as a mathematical problem solver. Saying he felt particularly strong one morning, he disappeared with a nasty equation that was perplexing Murph Goldberger and me, and returned with the solution in twenty minutes. I cannot imagine what it must feel like to be able to think with that rapidity and clarity in mathematics.

When Murray Gell-Mann arrived in Paris he came directly to our basement. Michel and I explained the problem we were working on and the next morning Gell-Mann reappeared, announcing in his perfect French, "Messieurs, le problème est résolu."

When Nobel Prize winners T. D. Lee and C. N. Yang (on the left and right, respectively) made my simple question about the hyperfine effect into a real scientific discovery and gave me equal credit as author on the paper, I was so happy I nearly jumped in the air.

April 8, 1959

Dr. Jeremy Bernstein
Institute for Advanced Study
Princeton, New Jersey

Dear Dr. Bernstein:

Your letter to Dr. Goudsmit of March 19 has
been referred to me. It will be possible to discuss
the matter of a position for a year hence in reasonable
detail when you come here in August.

It is clear an offer will be made to you, but
it is premature to discuss precise details. Salary levels
are bound to change for one thing. Perhaps you might find
the enclosed staff policy statement of interest. As a
guide an appropriate offer at the present time would be
as an Assistant Physicist for two years as an initial term
with a threshold salary somewhere at or above seven hundred
per month. I would be happy to discuss this by phone if
you wish to call collect in the near future.

Sincerely yours,

R. Christian Anderson
Assistant Director

RCA/ca
enclosure

*The position I accepted with the Brookhaven National Labora-
tory was the most joblike job I had ever been offered, and
they were willing to let me take the year in France to use the
National Science Foundation Fellowship I had just won. With
my return would also begin my career as a professional writer
with the publication in* The New Yorker *of "Letter from
Corsica."*

tried to establish was that Oppenheimer's attitude had an adverse impact on recruiting at places like Livermore. The witness previous to Teller that day, Kenneth Sanborn Pitzer, who was a professor of chemistry at Berkeley, was asked, "Doctor, is it or is it not true in your opinion that in the case of a scientist as influential as Dr. Oppenheimer, a failure to lend enthusiasm and vigorous support to a program might constitute hindrance to the program or opposition to the program?" Pitzer answered, "There is a certain element of semantics in that question, but I would say yes." Then it was Teller's turn. I have read Teller's testimony many times, and have always marvelled at the apparently guileless fashion in which he attacked Oppenheimer. It was a remarkable performance. Take, for instance, this exchange between Roger Robb and Teller:

> Q. To simplify the issues here, perhaps, let me ask you this question: Is it your intention, in anything that you are about to testify to, to suggest that Dr. Oppenheimer is disloyal to the United States?
>
> A. I do not want to suggest anything of the kind. I know Oppenheimer as an intellectually most alert and a very complicated person, and I think it would be presumptuous and wrong on my part if I would try in any way to analyze his motives. But I have always assumed, and I now assume, that he is loyal to the United States. I believe this, and I shall believe it until I see very conclusive proof to the opposite.
>
> Q. Now, a question which is the corollary of that. Do you or do you not believe that Dr. Oppenheimer is a security risk?
>
> A. In a great number of cases I have seen Dr. Oppenheimer act — I understood that Dr. Oppenheimer acted — in a way which for me was exceedingly hard to understand. I thoroughly disagreed with him on numerous issues, and his actions frankly appeared to me confused and complicated. To this extent, I feel that I would like to see the vital interests of this country in hands which I understand better and therefore trust more.

When the matter of the recruiting came up, Teller was able to assure the committee that Karplus was on board. He was asked, "Did you have any difficulty recruiting personnel for that laboratory?" He answered, "Yes, but not terribly difficult." Then he was asked, "Did you get the personnel you needed?" Teller answered, "This is a question I cannot really answer, because it is always possible to get better personnel. But I am very happy about the people whom we did get and we are still looking for very excellent people if we can get them, and I am going to spend the next three days in the Physical Society in trying to persuade additional young people to join us." It must have been during one of those days that I met Teller. I have been grateful ever since that I was not persuaded to go to Livermore.

The following year went uneventfully. My thesis worked its way toward completion. I had no more job offers, but for some reason this did not worry me. It was not that I shouldn't have worried; it is just that I didn't. (Indeed, for the next seven years, I was not to have a job that had tenure beyond a single year. I never knew what I would be doing the following year, or where, and I got used to the uncertainty.) As it turned out, I backed into an absolutely perfect job. A few years earlier the Harvard Cyclotron had created a post called the "house theoretician." The position carried no very explicit duties; the incumbent was to be available to experimenters to discuss anything they might have in mind. The rest of the time he could do his own research. During the time I was writing my thesis the job had been held by a man named Bertram Malenka, who had taken his degree with Schwinger in 1951. Just at the time I was finishing my thesis, Malenka left for Washington University in St. Louis, and with the help of Gerald Holton, I got the job. There were no prescribed hours, and during the two years I spent there — my one-year appointment was renewed — I can remember only one occasion when an experimental physicist asked me anything. The

Harvard experimental physicists knew as much theory as I did.

I did, however, have a research program. By this time I knew a good deal about the deuteron, and more was being discovered in experiments being carried out at Stanford University. Electrons were beamed on to deuterons, whose shape determined the resulting collision. This constituted the first direct measurement of the deuteron's shape. I wrote several papers about the analysis of this experiment and got to teach the subject in a nuclear physics course when its professor, Norman Ramsey, was called to Washington to debate McCarthy on national television. I recall those two years as being among the happiest of my early life. When they were over, it was understood that I would move on and open up the job for someone else. There was one place in all the world I wanted to go, and that was the Institute for Advanced Study at Princeton.

The Institute had been created in Princeton in 1930, the idea of the educator Abraham Flexner, who wanted an environment in which outstanding young scholars could be in close contact with acknowledged masters in their fields. His first appointment as professor was Einstein, who came in 1933. Flexner thought the first members should be in mathematics and theoretical physics, since practitioners of these disciplines require a minimum of technological support — essentially none until the introduction of computers. The institute occupied a few offices in the university until 1940 when it moved to a new campus a few miles out of town. While still a graduate student I had visited a friend there. The first evening, as we were driving to town, he pointed out the figure of Einstein walking slowly toward his house on Mercer Street. It was the only time I ever saw him.

Although Einstein had died in 1955, I still thought of

the Institute as his. Going there was a very prestigious thing for a young physicist to do. I had heard Oppenheimer speak, had read what he had written, and was extremely impressed by him; to me he was an intellectual hero. By this time, too, I had gotten to know Schwinger reasonably well. The small group of theorists in Cambridge used to eat together every Wednesday noon at Chez Dreyfus, where Schwinger would sketch his latest discoveries on napkins or place mats. It was an extraordinarily exciting thing to witness. I had used Schwinger's ideas in a couple of my papers, and he had been very helpful in explaining them. So I went to him and asked whether he would write a letter for me to Oppenheimer. I remember adding irreverently, "The next time I'll do the same for you." He wrote, as did a few other Cambridge colleagues, and late in April I learned that I had been accepted as a one-year visitor. I have never been so elated.

During the time I was a graduate student Philipp Frank retired. We had never lost touch and often talked together. Professor Frank turned seventy in 1954, and I know that in his last years he was deeply hurt because the department had taken away his relativity course and given it to a younger man. It is true that his course was pretty slow-moving and probably somewhat out of date, but it had a quality of scholarship that no young person could re-create. At the time of his retirement, Frank was asked to clean out his office, and I helped him at the sad task. The room was an ungodly mess. Professor Frank explained the distinction between his wife's "linear order" and his own more subtle order, of which the office was supposed to be an illustration. He had an old roll-top desk in which we found a slew of unopened and unanswered letters, some dating back at least a decade. We opened several of them, and Professor Frank commented that they "weren't so important anyway." There were letters from Einstein that Philipp had read and saved; these were stuffed in drawers, along with letters from other distinguished physicists and philosophers. It was a priceless collection, most of which seems to have disappeared. He turned up a scroll-like object, covered with dust, that turned out to be an etching of Einstein done in 1931 and signed by both the subject and the artist. Professor Frank asked me whether I would like it; it now hangs on my wall.

The last time I saw the Franks was ten years later. I went with Gerald Holton to discuss their moving into a retirement home Holton had found, which would be more suitable for their needs. Holton had a copy of a new book that contained some of Professor Frank's essays. Philipp looked at it for a bit. Then he said, partly to himself and partly to us, that it was as if these essays had been written by somebody else. He died on July 21, 1966.

5

Though
Every Prospect Pleases

I ARRIVED at the Institute for Advanced Study in Princeton in the fall of 1957, after nearly ten years at Harvard. Not long after I got there, I went to a party given by the local physicists and their wives. Among the guests was Freeman Dyson, who was already a permanent member of the Institute. One of the wives asked Dyson what he thought, in a general way, of Princeton. Without batting an eyelash, Dyson responded, "Though every prospect pleases and only man is vile."

Although I was extremely impressed by its literary aptness, I was not sure quite what to make of Dyson's answer. It was years before I came to realize that nothing Dyson says can be entirely anticipated, and more years before I finally nailed down the quotation. It is from a hymn — "From Greenland's Icy Mountains" — that, Dyson later explained, he often had sung in chapel at Winchester, his public school. At the time, I was not quite sure what to make of the Institute, either. One of my professors at Harvard had said that to tell anyone there about an idea before one had published it was like "throwing a silver coin among a den of thieves." Another warned me about Robert Oppenheimer's weekly "confessionals," at which all the temporary members were expected to say what they had accomplished by way of research the preceding week. I was told that it was all right to say that you had done nothing, but if you claimed to have done something that turned out to be either wrong or trivial, you were done for. I had decided, given this advice, that I would say nothing to anyone. When I explained my tactic to Julian Schwinger, he remarked kindly, "That may keep you out of trouble."

I actually arrived at Princeton via Los Alamos, where I had spent the summer. The Los Alamos Laboratory was then actively recruiting young physicists, and I found the idea of spending a summer in New Mexico immensely appealing. It is difficult to believe now, but most young physicists at that time, like me, had no reluctance about working at a place whose principal mission was to design and construct nuclear weapons. I feel I should make this clear, and not try to attribute values to myself when young that I acquired only later. In fact, my main concern was that I might not get my Q clearance, the highest form of government clearance, required for anyone working in a weapons laboratory. This was the tail end of the McCarthy period, and I had a great-aunt who was an avid reader of the *Daily Worker*. She was such an iconoclast that it is difficult to believe she actually belonged to anything, but I was afraid that the FBI would find out — they probably already knew — that she was, at once, my great-aunt and a subscriber to the *Worker*, and that that would queer my summer in New Mexico. Some FBI people did interview me and my friends and neighbors, and to my relief I was cleared.

Los Alamos was then an entirely closed city, encircled by barbed wire and set in wildly beautiful natural surroundings. I was both poor and single. As a consequence of the former, I had no car but did manage to buy a serviceable red bicycle. As a consequence of the latter, I was housed in a primitive wooden dormitory that was surely a residue of the war, during which it may well have housed several Nobel Prize winners. I shared an office in the theoretical building — a few miles away and up a hill — with a brilliant, equally young former Schwinger student named Kenneth Johnson, who is now a professor at MIT. Our office was tucked away in a kind of aerie far from the main offices. No one seemed to have any work for us to do, so we spent our time doing whatever was left of the physics problems we had been working on at Harvard the previous winter. Our tranquillity was interrupted a few weeks later when a galaxy of superstars in theoretical physics appeared at the laboratory. They were going to work on controlled nuclear fusion — the use of the fusion of light elements to produce nuclear power — something that was then a classified project and that now, as an open research project, is the focus of a huge amount of successful activity. Among the newcomers was one of America's most gifted theoretical physicists, Francis Low. The friendship I developed with him that summer — and it has lasted nearly thirty years — played a decisive part in whatever firsthand knowledge I have of the effects of nuclear weapons.

Francis celebrated his sixtieth birthday in 1981, while he was provost of MIT. A group of us produced a birthday book for him, and in it I told of the weekend when Francis and I went to Nevada to watch the atomic bombs. Put that way, the trip sounds frivolous and, in a way, it was.

Although all of us had our Q clearances, we were, effectively, divided into two classes — what I used to think of as the adult world and the child's world. The adults, of which I was not one, knew the "secret" — the secret of the hydrogen bomb. The children didn't know it and were — or so I felt — not going to know it until we became adults; i.e., until we actually began working on weapons. The bomb was a kind of eerie presence that hung over the laboratory. It was never discussed openly, at least within my earshot. There were rumors that several bombs were stored in a cave, specially lit and guarded, just below the mesa. It was also rumored that if you knew the secret, your travel abroad would be restricted so that you would not be in a position to pass it to anyone else. This was the time when bombs were being routinely tested in the atmosphere, and you might come across a group of colleagues arcanely discussing the results of a test with some name like Newton or Kepler. I picked up odd bits of information, like the word "shake." This was a unit of time — I can no longer remember whether it was a nanosecond or more, although "shorter than two shakes of a lamb's tail" was the origin — that separated one shock-wave signal from the detonation of a hydrogen bomb from the next. There is a sequence — fission explosion, fusion explosion, and fission explosion — each one separated from the other by several shakes, which is how, it was explained to me, one can distinguish their seismic signal from an earthquake.

Francis and I played innumerable games of tennis. He was very athletic and probably the only physicist to have served in the ski troops during the war. One day, after a game, Francis told me that the following weekend he was going to Mercury, Nevada, to see the atomic bombs. I naturally assumed that he was on assignment from the adult world, and it was only years later when we were discussing it that he told me that, like me, he had gone out of simple curiosity. Francis suggested that I ask our division leader, Carson Mark, whether I could go along, too. Mark, an amiable Canadian who had been at Los Alamos since the war, was agreeable, provided I pay for my own transportation; he did not see any reason that my weekend should be subsidized by the Atomic Energy Commission. Thus, the three of us found ourselves in a small plane that took us from Los Alamos to Albuquerque, where we boarded a commercial airliner for the trip to Las Vegas.

In Francis's birthday book I described how we arrived in Las Vegas around nine in the evening and went immediately to a large gambling casino. Some mathematicians had just made a complete analysis of the casino game of blackjack — in which the dealer is, in effect, an automaton — and had devised a theoretical scheme that, if you could remember it, would guarantee your losing money at the slowest possible rate. You could actually win over the long run. The strategy had been tried at Los Alamos — hundreds of thousands of games were played — on one of the large computers when it was not doing weapons calculations. The results were summarized on a pocket card we had with us, and when we arrived at the casino, we headed for the blackjack tables and spent the next several hours applying the scheme, with marginal degrees of success.

It had been arranged with the casino that if an atomic bomb test scheduled for the following morning was to take place, the casino would turn on a blue light, and at about one in the morning all the Los Alamos personnel would head back to Mercury, the actual test site. On the night we arrived, the light was on, so at about one, in the pitch dark, we drove through the barren Nevada countryside to Mercury. The bombs went off at sunrise, apparently so that the photographers could capture the explosions on film. I managed to get a brief nap on a cot in the main test control center before someone woke me up to say we were to go outside. It was very dark and very cold. I could make out enough to see that the countryside was basically a desert. We stood in a small, shivering group while Carson Mark distributed smoked glasses and told us to face away from the explosion, which, glasses or no, would otherwise blind us. Someone counted over a loudspeaker backward from ten to zero. There was a flash of light and after a few seconds we all turned around. My first thought — and this seems to have been common to many people who saw those tests — was "My God, that's beautiful." An orange-red-rose cloud was rising out of the desert, and it *was* beautiful. Then it cooled, turning darker and darker — a purple-black menacing color. As Robert Oppenheimer remembered from the *Bhagavad-Gita* after the first bomb explosion:

> I am become Death
> The destroyer of worlds.

After we had had a few hours of sleep, Carson Mark gave us a tour of the site. We drove past the desert land where earlier tests had taken place. Nothing was growing; the ground seemed fused, like the surface of the moon. Signs indicated where the radiation level was still high, and we closed the windows of the car to keep out the radioactive air. It was very still. I had never experienced such absolute silence. We stopped at a tower where they were installing the bomb — Galileo — for next morning's test, and we climbed to the swaying top, several hundred feet above the desert, and watched them put together the pieces of the bomb assembly. Everything was hushed, almost noiseless; the only sound was the clicking of some vacuum pumps. Then we were taken to a small, low building, all in heavy concrete and set away from the rest. Carson Mark opened the door — and what I saw caused me to start backward. It was one room filled entirely with atomic bombs and parts of atomic bombs — enough, no doubt, to destroy a continent. The heart of the bomb is a perfect sphere of plutonium or uranium, about the size and weight of a bowling ball. I was given one to hold in both hands. Don't drop it. It was warm — it gave off warmth, radioactivity.

When Francis and I exchanged our memories of this visit, I discovered that I had misremembered some of the chronology. In particular, we could not agree as to whether or not *she* had been there. There was a woman in the blockhouse, I said, who sat knitting while a man — a husband or a boyfriend — filed on the high explosive that was wrapped around the "pits," the metal sphere that was the heart of the bomb. As I talked to Francis, and as I write this now, I see her there, dressed in a sweater and a skirt, knitting intently while the man filed on a bomb. What was she doing there? I don't know and didn't ask. Francis did not remember her. I wrote to Carson Mark, and he didn't remember her, either. But I *know* she was there. It somehow became the meaning to me of the whole visit . . . though every prospect pleases. Only a few months ago I saw Francis at someone else's sixtieth birthday party. We hadn't seen each other for a while and talked of this and that. Suddenly he looked at me and said, "You were right. One morning I woke up and I had an absolutely clear vision of that scene. She *was* there."

As I reread what I have just written, I am afraid that it may give the impression that I was made wise — instantaneously wise — by seeing the bombs; I mean wise about atomic bombs. I was not made wise. I was made foolish. I had not completely entered the adult world; I still did not know the secret. But I had seen bombs explode and I had held one in my hands. The effect of this was to give me a feeling of power to which I was not entitled. I wanted the aboveground testing to go on. I thought that it was all very important and necessary. I thought that if Adlai Stevenson, who had run against Eisenhower the previous year on a platform that included the abolition of aboveground testing, could only come to Mercury, he too would see how important and necessary it all was. I thought that if I could get to see him, I could convince him that he had been wrong. There are times in life when it is better not to get what one wishes for, and this was certainly one of those times.

As it happened I was then going out with a girl who lived in Lake Forest, Illinois, and whose family knew Adlai Stevenson. I had arranged to stop over and visit them on my way back east to Princeton. Francis and I drove in his car as far as Lake Forest, where he dropped me off. At dinner I told my girlfriend's mother about the bomb tests and what I took to be their great importance. I knew so little about weapons technology that I can't imagine what I could have told her about the importance of the tests and what I could have said about the need to test in the atmosphere. In retrospect, that seems so crazy to me that I can't imagine what I said. Yet she was enough impressed to believe that it was just what Adlai Stevenson needed to hear.

The next day we went for cocktails to Stevenson's

home in Libertyville. After some social chitchat, my friend's mother withdrew, leaving me with my host, and I began my spiel. After I had spoken a few sentences, Stevenson got up and walked away. He said nothing. He just walked away. I was terribly embarrassed. He had heard enough foolishness on this subject from "experts," and he did not want to hear any more, and in his house at that, from the likes of me. By this time — 1957 — the responsible scientists were already beginning to agitate for a test ban, which was eventually endorsed by Eisenhower but was not signed until 1963, by Kennedy, and then in a limited form.

Before I went to Princeton I had met Oppenheimer, face to face, only once. The experience had given me some sense of the complexity of his character. Our encounter occurred in the spring of 1957, just before my summer at Los Alamos.

All the time I was studying physics — first as an undergraduate, then as a graduate, and then as a postdoctoral student — I was quite sure that each of these steps would be the last for me. I was, I thought, surrounded by brilliant people — some near geniuses and a few real geniuses, like Schwinger — and I just didn't see how I was going to play any large role in the subject. That I would actually get to go to the Institute for Advanced Study, which was in those days unique as a center for postdoctoral study in theoretical physics, seemed so unlikely that I applied almost as a joke . . . a private joke. Not long after I got accepted Oppenheimer came to Harvard to deliver a series of public lectures.

Sanders Theatre, where the lectures were given, was filled to capacity. It must be difficult for physicists of the

present generation to imagine what a presence Oppenheimer was in our field, and what an electrifying public
figure. His use of language was somewhat opaque, often
poetic, and he had an odd, clipped diction that com-
manded attention. Yet I do not have the foggiest recollection of what he said except that in the last lecture he dealt
with the revolution wrought in our thinking by quantum
mechanics. I was seated directly behind two of those classic blue-haired Boston dowagers who look fragile but, I
am sure, will outlive us all. A gentle aroma of violets
floated around them. Oppenheimer had a small blackboard on the stage. At one point he said that to make
things precise he would write down the fact that in quantum mechanics the position and momentum don't "commute." It is not important to know what that means; very
few people in his audience knew. He took a chalk and
carefully wrote $qp - pq = i\hbar$. The two ladies clutched
each other for reassurance. Perhaps they thought that the
formula was going to explode. I was tempted to lean over
and tell them that it was all right — that Oppenheimer
was just showing off a bit — but I didn't, because it would
have destroyed the beauty of the moment.

After the lecture, thinking it might not be unreason-
able to say hello, since I was about to come to his Institute, I went to the speaker's platform. There was a line of
admirers and I waited my turn. When I introduced myself, Oppenheimer stared flatly at me. His extraordinary
blue eyes on this occasion looked like ice. I don't know
whether his look was actively hostile, but it certainly
wasn't friendly. Before retreating in total confusion, I
managed to say that I had just been accepted by his Institute and would be in Princeton in a few months. A transformation came over him. His face lit up like a sunrise.

He started telling me about the people who would also be visiting the Institute that fall: P. A. M. Dirac, Niels Bohr, T. D. Lee, C. N. Yang, and on and on. It sounded like the guest list at a Nobel Prize banquet. When he finished, he said, "Lee and Yang are going to teach us about parity violation and we are going to have a ball." "Have a ball": those were his exact words. I can hear them as I write this. I went away, walking on air.

My first day at the Institute was not an entirely auspicious one. I had driven from my parents' home in Rochester, where, with the proceeds of the summer, I had purchased an nth-hand Morris Minor convertible. It was only after the first rainstorm, en route, that I discovered that its ancient top leaked like a sieve. I stopped along the way to ask several people for directions, and arrived at the Institute soaking wet and absolutely filthy. My only thought was to get the keys to what my acceptance brochure had described as my "garden apartment," and go there immediately to take a bath.

I went to what looked like the main building, where I was directed to a large office, and tried to avoid touching anything for fear I would rub off on it. A secretary gave me some keys and then said that Oppenheimer wanted to see me. This seemed very unlikely under the best of circumstances and inconceivable in the present one. No, she insisted, Oppenheimer wanted to see me as soon as I arrived. I went into his office. He was, as was usually the case, dressed in one of the hand-tailored suits he had made at Langrocks, the local bespoke tailor. Much later the proprietor of Langrocks told me that Oppenheimer also had a specially tailored green loden coat that was cut long, like a cape. He was, certainly by physicists' standards, a well-to-do man, and he knew how to enjoy his money.

He looked at me amiably with those remarkable eyes and waited for me to say something. There was a horrible silence. The only thing I could think of to say was that I had just come from Los Alamos. He had lost his clearance in 1954, after the security hearings, and, I imagine, had not been back to Los Alamos since then. There was more silence and then he asked, "What's new and firm in physics?" The use of the word "firm" was, in that context, vintage Oppenheimer. I am not sure I could answer the question now, after working for nearly thirty years in the field. I said absolutely nothing, and he began a brief discussion of the latest news on the work that had followed the discovery of parity non-conservation by Lee and Yang. As it happened, I knew nothing about it, because I had been working in a completely different branch of elementary particle physics. Again I said nothing. By this time Oppenheimer must have decided that he was dealing with a cipher, and he dismissed me after extending an unusual invitation. Pointing vaguely in the direction of the director's mansion, he said that he and "Kitty" — his wife, whom I had never met — had a "small collection of pictures" and that I might come over and look at them some time. I thanked him for the invitation. Much later, on my first visit to his house, I noticed that the small collection included, among other things, a Van Gogh. I believe that he had inherited the collection from his father and had never added anything to it.

I found my way to the "garden apartment." It was the most splendid dwelling I had lived in in my adult life, most of which had been spent in college dormitories and student rooming houses. Oppenheimer told me later that he had personally selected the furnishings, right down to the ashtrays from Knoll's. The next day, much improved by a night's sleep, I went in search of my office. The physicists were then distributed in two Georgian-style red brick buildings. Dyson and former ambassador George Kennan had their offices in what became my building; Lee and Yang were in the other. In the main building, where Einstein's office had been, the distinguished Danish astronomer Bengt Strömgren had just been installed to begin a new astronomy program at the Institute. The younger people all had officemates, and as far as I could tell, none of the visitors had a telephone in his office. My officemate was a young Italian physicist, Giacomo Morpurgo, now a distinguished professor at the University of Genoa in Italy. After we had exchanged a few words I got down to my most pressing problem — how to stay out of the army. All during graduate school and my two years at the Harvard Cyclotron, I had been consistently deferred on the grounds that I was in an essential profession — a profession in which I was, needless to say, an absolute novice. Ironically, now that I was about to begin my real career in physics, the army had decided to draft me. This was a severe blow. Being away from physics for two or more years, especially the kind of physics I was trying to do — elementary particles, a field that was then changing every few weeks — would probably end my career. I was not even sure whether the Institute would take me back. And I had no other job prospects.

I decided that, despite the odd impression I must have made the previous day, the only thing to do was discuss the situation with Oppenheimer. I went to his office with my draft notice, but I didn't get beyond his secretary. Mine, it turned out, was a routine case. Oppenheimer must have been spending half his time writing to the draft boards of his young charges. The next day I was given a copy of his letter. It was two pages long. In one and seven-tenths pages he wrote a brilliant summary of modern physics from Einstein and Bohr to the present — the "excellences of physics." The last sentence said something like "Dr. Bernstein has now joined us to continue in this activity." It was almost the only mention of me in the entire letter. It was a con job but one on a very high level and for what I felt was an extremely good cause — my career in physics. Whatever it was, it worked. I was reclassified for a year.

That having been taken care of, I now had to figure out what to do with my time. My appointment was for one year. There was no guidance as to what one was meant to do during that year, nor was there any mention of a second year. But I had been functioning this way for the two years since I had gotten my Ph.D., and it seemed to me perfectly natural. Although I had assumed at every stage that my career in physics would come to an end, I had not given a great deal of thought as to what I would do when it did — perhaps take up computer programming, a field that at the time seemed to have some future. As it happened, while I was at Los Alamos Francis Low had introduced me to his friend and colleague Marvin L. Goldberger, known to all of us as Murph. Murph has been president of the California Institute of Technology for nearly a decade, but when I first met him he had just moved from the University of Chicago to Princeton, where he taught until he went to Cal Tech. Apart from being a superb theoretical physicist, Murph is one of the funniest people I know. He loves to laugh and so do I, and we hit it off at once. We were also working in the same area — the electromagnetic interaction of electrons with other elementary particles. This was a hot field at the time. In fact, Murph went on to invent the basic technique, the so-called dispersion relations, which became the standard way of dealing with these phenomena. He had suggested that summer that I look him up when I got to Princeton so that we might do some work together.

I called him and, typically, he immediately invited me over for dinner. In the next few days Murph and I set to work, and not long afterward I got my first view of Freeman Dyson as a mathematical problem solver. It was early in the morning — by Institute standards. Most people worked at night and were not seen until after noon. Murph had come up with a nasty-looking integral equation. It doesn't matter much what that is except that it was nasty. He had divided the terms into two groups; one was labeled $G(x)$, for "good of x," and the other was labeled $H(x)$, for "horrible of x." We were standing at the blackboard, staring morosely at horrible of x, when Dyson came in with his morning cup of coffee. He studied our equation. Murph asked, "Freeman, have you ever seen one like this?" Dyson said no, but that he felt particularly strong that morning. He copied down our equation and disappeared. In about twenty minutes he was back with the solution. It was rediscovered by other people later and bears their names, but I saw what seemed to me, and still seems to me, like an incomprehensible conjuring trick. Over the years I have watched Dyson solve many different kinds of mathematical problems, and I cannot imagine what it must feel like to be able to think with that rapidity and clarity in mathematics. Does everyone else appear to be going in slow motion? It is something that surely cannot be taught, at least to me.

But I have learned enough mathematics to get pleasure and delight each time I see it happen.

Goldberger and I, after working for a couple of months, produced a review article — a mixture of original work and review — that summarized what we knew and what was known about the electron interactions with particles like protons and neutrons. By this time this field had already moved out of the mainstream of the physics being done at the Institute and elsewhere, which had to do with exploring the consequences of the revolution wrought by Lee and Yang: the discovery that many of the cherished symmetry principles of physics have only limited validity, a discovery we still do not understand on a fundamental level. Each week Lee or Yang gave a lecture that summarized where things stood. If the truth be told, I paid little attention to them. In part, this was because I was working with Murph on something else, in part because I was lazy, and in part because Oppenheimer had assigned me a task that took up a good deal of my time.

As I have mentioned, the Institute had decided to move into astronomy and had just appointed Bengt Strömgren. Oppenheimer decided that we all needed to learn something about the subject. This was before the modern Big Bang theory — quasars and pulsars and the rest. While I was at Harvard I had taken a course in classical astronomy, had found it dull, and had promptly forgotten it. But Oppenheimer made it quite plain that the junior members were meant to attend Strömgren's lectures on a regular basis. In fact, the lectures were willingly attended by everybody. I listened to the first one in a kind of stupor, deeply absorbed by something I was doing with Murph. My trance rapidly dissipated when I heard my name mentioned. Oppenheimer announced that there would be printed notes distributed and, to my horror, that I was to write them when I had a chance. After the lecture I explained to Oppenheimer that I knew nothing about astronomy. He said, "Good, this will give you a chance to learn it." I. I. Rabi once told me, when he was a young postdoc he was asked by the great Otto Stern to do a certain experiment. "They told me that it was an honor," he said, "and I was in no position to refuse an honor." I decided that I would keep my mouth shut and do the notes. Fortunately, Strömgren understood the situation. After every lecture he gave me a meticulous set of his own handwritten notes, and I had very little to do except see that they were printed and ready each week. I hope they did some good. At last report Strömgren had gone to Denmark, where he was living in the famous house that the Carlsberg beer people built for Bohr.

The social life at the Institute, as it was in 1957, is worth commenting on, since it was part of the ambience in which we did our work. There were three classes of physicists. First were the permanent members, like Dyson and Yang and, a little later, Lee. Then came a class of visitors whom Oppenheimer used to refer to as "our special friends" — people like Niels Bohr, P. A. M. Dirac, and Wolfgang Pauli, who were encouraged to visit whenever it was convenient for them. Dirac was in residence that year, and Bohr appeared from time to time. Then there were the temporary members, who were themselves divided into two groups. Most were people of distinction who had permanent jobs at famous universities and were visiting the Institute on sabbatical. They did not have to worry about their future employment; if they ended up doing nothing during their entire Institute year they could nonetheless return, refreshed, to places like Har-

vard, Stanford, and Berkeley. The rest of us, who had neither jobs nor reputations, were under a good deal of psy-
chological pressure to produce something. Some of the
people in this category found the strain too great. One of
my predecessors from Harvard simply walked out of the
Institute in midsemester and joined a monastic order. He
is now married to a former nun and, when I saw him last,
had returned to physics. My own response to the pressure
was very simple. Since I had always assumed that I had
no future in physics, I decided that I might as well enjoy
myself and wait to see what, if anything, would happen.

I was fortunate in finding a colleague who seemed to
be in the same boat and have roughly the same attitude.
Michael Cohen, now a professor at the University of Pennsylvania, is one of the great eccentric wits in physics. He
had been one of Feynman's few students and had produced
a brilliant thesis. Having been in proximity to the master
for several years, Cohen, who was an uncannily accurate
mimic, could do Feynman to a T. This ability was put to
use a few years later, when Cohen's tenure was being
decided at Pennsylvania. The deliberations of the sitting
committee were interrupted by a call from Cal Tech. It
was Feynman. At this time the university was interested
in luring Feynman east, so one of the members of the committee eagerly went to the telephone. A conversation
ensued which ended when Feynman said that one of the
reasons he was thinking seriously about shifting to Pennsylvania was that the move would give him a chance to
renew his collaboration with his former student Cohen.
This was too much, and Cohen's jape was uncovered. He
got tenure anyway.

If I had had any tendency to pretentiousness, an hour
with Cohen would have dealt with it. We used to take

walks in the woods just out of sight of the Institute. When we were safely out of earshot of our elders and betters, we would commiserate about some of Oppenheimer's more baroque mannerisms. After Cohen learned that I had been the house theorist at the Harvard Cyclotron, he remarked, "There are the house theorists and the field theorists," an unfavorable comparison of my activity with that of the very powerful, mostly German-speaking field theorists who were also assembled at the Institute that fall. They were known as the Feldverein — roughly, the Field Theory Corporation. Dyson was working with them and after several weeks of what the distinguished Swiss physicist Res Jost referred to as "tutorial," he produced a basic paper on the mathematical foundations of quantum field theory.

Since Cohen and I thought of ourselves as being at the far infrared end of the local social spectrum, we were amazed to receive invitations to a party at the Oppenheimers'. At first we thought that this was one of those routine academic affairs where all faculty members with initials from A to M are invited on Wednesday to have tea with the president. However, discreet inquiries satisfied us that it wasn't so.

We showed up at the party together and realized, almost at once, that we were in over our heads. I recognized John O'Hara and the governor of New Jersey, among others, and saw none of our physics colleagues. No one had warned us about Oppenheimer's martinis. He mixed them very strong, I suppose to see what would happen. A factotum passed them out on a tray, and each time your glass was empty another tray would magically appear, with the odd hors d'oeuvre. Cohen and I admired Oppenheimer's paintings, had a couple of martinis, and then decided to get as far away from the action in the house as decency would allow. We found a quiet spot at the bottom of the Oppenheimers' garden. It was a lovely fall night and we settled next to a flower bed for a pleasant evening of conversation. From time to time the factotum would appear with his tray and each of us would have yet another martini. By now, every time I moved my head, constellations seemed to go into orbit. Cohen was lying face down, intently studying some sort of weed, when I spotted Oppenheimer and Kitty heading in our direction. It was midnight, and I suppose most of the other guests had gone home. I tried to alert Cohen that the Oppenheimers were in the vicinity and closing fast, but he did not seem interested. The matter became urgent when the Oppenheimers stood directly over Cohen. In an attempt to make conversation, Oppenheimer said, "Kitty, this is Michael Cohen. He comes to us from Feynman, Los Angeles, and many mutual friends." *This* caught Cohen's attention. He propped himself up on one elbow and said, amiably, "Yeah," at which Oppenheimer and his wife continued their walk. Somehow we got home. The next day Cohen came to me with the information that this had been the Oppenheimers' "fun" party and that we had been invited because the Oppenheimers thought we might be fun. "If I'd known," Cohen added, "I would have told some Jewish jokes." He had an essentially inexhaustible supply.

I invited Oppenheimer to a party of my own that year, and much to my astonishment he came. When I got word that he was coming, I alerted everyone and we all put on our best clothes. He showed up in a jacket with worn cuffs and elbow patches that must have been left over from his student days. I guess he felt that he would fit in better. Apart from the occasional party, the principal social activity was touch football. We played nearly every afternoon when the weather was good. It is hard to say whether this was before work or after work, because people's working hours were so idiosyncratic. There was a French mathematician, for example, who was experimenting with a twenty-five-hour day, which meant that his meal times had a secular drift with respect to the rest of us.

That year the mathematics section of the Institute — traditionally one of the strongest sections — was heavily weighted with French mathematicians, among them Jean Leray, a senior professor at the Collège de France, and J. P. Serre, his junior colleague, then regarded as one of the rising stars of French mathematics. For one reason or another, I found myself on the football team with the younger French mathematicians. We were distinguished by our great enthusiasm and nearly total lack of discipline. The only play I could get the group to run was what they called "*la Statue de la Liberté*." They liked the name. It was a sure loser, but we ran it again and again. On one occasion a teammate lost a contact lens and the game stopped while some twenty of us got down on our hands and knees to look for it. One of the onlookers — we usually attracted a crowd — was Leray. His curiosity aroused by the spectacle of all of us rooting around in the grass, he asked Serre what we were doing. Serre replied, "We are playing American football and we are looking for the ball." We must have made a lot of noise; soon afterward a notice appeared in the main building, over Oppenheimer's signature: "Members are kindly requested to play touch football out of earshot of the library."

A few weeks later I overheard an unforgettable conversation between Leray and a young American mathematician in the Institute cafeteria. ("Cafeteria" is a misleading word. Oppenheimer had elevated self-service to a new level — gourmet food on a tray. The "locals" were delighted to be invited to dinner at the Institute.) Leray, who as a rule said almost nothing, found himself seated next to a garrulous non-French-speaking American mathematician. The conversation went like this:

> MATHEMATICIAN: Professor Leray, do you go to the
> movies?
> LERAY: (Silence)
> MATHEMATICIAN: What do you think about gangster
> movies?
> LERAY: (Silence)

The mathematician, under the impression that the word "gangster" had eluded Leray, repeated it several times, pointing his fingers and making a loud popping sound. He then asked, "Professor Leray, do you have gangsters in France?" At this, Leray brightened and replied, in faultless English, "Yes, but they constitute the government."

Once a week there was the celebrated physics colloquium at the Institute. Not only did all the members attend but so did faculty, graduate students, and visitors from Princeton and elsewhere. The really "hot" colloquia were not announced publicly, to keep the attendance down, but word got around and the relatively small conference room would be filled to overflowing. Because it was near my office, I could time things to get a seat in the back. The front row was reserved for the *Geheimrats*, with Oppenheimer sitting in the middle. My proximity to the conference room and my propensity to work on weekends led to an interesting incident. One Saturday I came to work and found the nearby room alive with floodlights. A television newsman — I think it was Howard K. Smith — was interviewing Oppenheimer. I stuck my head in far enough to observe but not far enough, I thought, to be seen. What I witnessed revealed once again Oppie's complex character. When the cameras were rolling he spoke in a soft voice, his eyes lowered; he wore an almost martyred look. I think that he and Smith were discussing what he used to refer to contemptuously as his "case," the security trial. When the cameras stopped, there was a different Oppenheimer — the "smiling public man" — discussing with Smith the "in" French restaurants in New York and the Caribbean, where Oppie had a home. It was an eerie form of show business. At some point he caught sight of me and said I could watch so long as he couldn't see me — an odd request to which, of course, I agreed.

The year began with the colloquia of Lee and Yang. At the first one I noticed that there was an empty chair next to Oppenheimer. He explained that it was for Dirac. Dirac, who died in the fall of 1984, was one of the founders of the quantum theory and an acknowledged character. Most of the stories that have survived him have to do with his extraordinary laconism; he had almost a mania for saying all and *only* all the right things, not one word too many. The first time I saw him, the colloquium was under way, well under way, when the door opened and in walked Dirac. His white hair flew in every direction and he was wearing a blue suit and a gigantic pair of muddy boots. I later learned that he had just come back from his afternoon walk in the woods, where, with the aid of an ax, he was making a path in the general direction of Trenton. He looked like a character out of Shakespeare, a sort of wild, ancient genius. He was in fact one of the great geniuses of twentieth-century science, and although I thought he was terribly old, he was then fifty-six, the age I am as I write this. He sat down and listened to the speaker with a look of benign bemusement, saying nothing.

Sometimes at night Dirac would have dinner with a few of us. The only thing I recall his saying — perhaps it was the only thing he *did* say — came in a conversation I was having with another young physicist about one of our senior colleagues, who was supposed to have become very rich through consulting. He seemed to live simply, and that gave rise to the interesting question of what he did with his money. I raised the point with my friend, who was at the same university as this noted physicist. He said he thought the man invested his money, but that did not seem to me to solve the puzzle, because, as I pointed out, he would then simply earn *more* money. Dirac, who had been silent throughout our exchange, suddenly volunteered, "Perhaps he loses it."

As I have indicated, there were two main lines of work going on at the Institute. Most of the young people were engaged in following up the discoveries of Lee and Yang. These were evolving so rapidly that a colleague of mine remarked that he felt "like a very small dog chasing a very large truck." Most of the others, the Feldverein, were trying to sort out the foundations of quantum field theory, a herculean task that is still very far from completion. While I was working with Murph, I more or less ignored both schools. But when that work was over I was once again in the familiar situation of needing a new problem to work on. I thought that if somehow I could come up with a problem in the general area of the weak interactions — the sort of thing that Lee and Yang were doing — I could motivate myself to learn the discipline. (I find it hard to learn a new field of physics unless I am either teaching it or doing a problem in it.) What happened was more than I bargained for. The story requires a little knowledge of physics, though the important thing is not the physics but how the people involved interacted, how a scientific collaboration actually works.

It began when I was still the house theoretician at the Harvard Cyclotron. MIT had as a visitor the brilliant young Austrian theoretical physicist Walter Thirring. Thirring, now at the Boltzmann Institute in Vienna, is as responsible as anyone for reviving Austrian physics after the war. He was in his twenties when I met him and had already written a splendid monograph on quantum electrodynamics — the field theory of electrons, positrons, and photons. The paper had caught the eye of Victor Weisskopf at MIT, who compared it with the extraordinary monograph that Wolfgang Pauli had written on the theory of relativity when he was just twenty-one. Weisskopf decided that Thirring's book *had* to be translated into English and that I, despite my lack of expertise in German, was just the person to do the translation. He got Thirring and me together, and we prepared an English edition of the book. It was more than a translation, since Thirring added a lot of new things that I helped to write up. In the course of this work, Thirring gave me some of his papers to read. Among them was one that looked interesting but that I had never read carefully. I took it to Princeton with the idea of reading it there.

Thirring's paper had to do with what is called the hyperfine interaction. This is the magnetic interaction between two spinning particles, which can cause small displacements in the electromagnetic spectra of atoms. The point is that in normal atoms it is a small effect. But Thirring noticed that if the electron in the atom was replaced by a much heavier particle, the hyperfine effect could become large. It was this point which I had in my head, although I really was not sure precisely how the hyperfine effect was calculated; the fact is, I did not know much about the subject at all. Just about the time I was working through Thirring's paper, Lee and Yang, in collaboration with an old friend of mine, Kerson Huang of MIT, produced a prepublication version of a brief paper they had written about the capture of mu mesons — very heavy electrons — by the proton. They worked so fast that, I was told, their entire paper was written on a train trip from Rochester, where they had been to a conference, to New York. The general subject of muon capture was well known, but they were bringing it up to date with the new theory.

When I looked at the Lee, Yang, and Huang paper, it occurred to me that because of the mu meson's large mass, Thirring's observation might have some relevance. I had no idea *what* relevance, but this seemed a good reason for me to begin to study Lee and Yang's work. This notion came to me on a beautiful Sunday morning in the winter. As it happened I had a date with a cousin of Michael Cohen's in New York for late Sunday afternoon. With my ancient car, I counted on about an hour and a half to drive to her house from Princeton, so I thought that if I left by one o'clock I would have plenty of time. This gave me a couple of hours to go to the Institute, fish out the paper by Lee, Yang, and Huang, and see whether *they* had treated the hyperfine effect. I looked through the paper carefully and found no mention. My next thought was to go over to the Institute library and get a book that discussed the hyperfine effect in detail so that I could learn about it. As I was heading across the snowy lawn, I saw T. D. Lee walking toward his office. I knew him only casually then — he has since become one of my closest friends — but I thought he would not mind if I asked him about the hyperfine effect. He might well have considered it and found that it was not interesting, thereby saving me, I reasoned, a great deal of useless work. When I asked, Lee said that he and the others had not considered it but that, offhand, he did not think the hyperfine effect would make much difference. I asked whether he'd mind explaining that to me in more detail, and we went to his office, where he started computing in his beautiful, almost calligraphic handwriting on the blackboard. As he computed, he carried on a running dialogue both with himself and me. The more he computed, the more animated grew the dialogue and the clearer it became that a relatively large scientific fish was in the process of being caught. He had turned my inchoate question into what seemed to be the beginning of real scientific discovery. Meanwhile, I was sneaking glances at my watch, and at about one-thirty I told Lee that I had to leave. I figured that if I was late, I could tell Cohen's cousin that it isn't every day one gets to work with a Nobel Prize winner. Lee and Yang had won theirs that very year.

I returned to Princeton late that night and by the time I got to my office the next day it was close to noon. We had pigeonhole mailboxes near the entrance to the building and in mine I found a note from Lee, asking me to call him. I did so at once, and he informed me that Yang was now actively engaged in the problem, and that they had drafted the beginnings of a paper that he wanted me to see. They must have worked all night. I went to his office, and he handed me several typewritten sheets and asked me to call him after I had read them. When I looked at the first page of the paper in the privacy of my office, I was so happy that I nearly jumped in the air. My name appeared as one of the three authors, and the names were in alphabetical order. This latter was important; any departure from alphabetical order usually indicates an unequal distribution of credit. What Lee and Yang had done was much more — much, much more — than the ethics of the situation required: they had made my naïve question into a scientific argument. I do not think that I would ever have been able to do the complete job they did, and I would have been very satisfied if they had simply thanked me in a footnote for asking the question, a common occurrence in physics papers. I was an unknown physicist and they were at the zenith of their profession. Their kindness was an act of generosity that I shall never forget.

I had been given the agreeable task of checking the formulae, but my work was interrupted because the American Physical Society was about to meet in New York. I had no job for the next year, so it behooved me to go to the meeting to see whether I could find a job somewhere. By this time Cohen and I were "candleing" each other's mail — holding it up to the light to see whether the other had been offered a job. This practice was known to one and all and was accepted as a given; the mail was readily accessible in the open boxes. However, I underestimated Cohen. On reaching the meeting, I went immediately to the large message board with the hope, unfulfilled, that there would be a note from some department chairman suggesting an interview. Of course, I looked under Cohen's name as well. There was indeed a message for him and, needless to say, I read it. It was from Robert Bacher, then chairman of the Cal Tech physics department. It said that he and Cohen might have some things of mutual interest to discuss, and suggested a meeting place and time. I saw Cohen several times at the meeting, but he said nothing about Bacher's message. I asked whether he had had any nibbles but elicited nothing. When I got back to the Institute, I asked whether anyone had heard about Cohen's getting an offer from Cal Tech. Different people said different things, which only heightened my curiosity. Finally, I confronted Cohen. He burst into triumphant peals of laughter. He had planted the note and had then informed everyone at the Institute, feeding them lines to use on me. I think he even got Dyson into the act. It worked — but I continued to candle his mail.

In addition to looking for a job, at which I was totally unsuccessful, my mission at the meeting was to find an experimenter working with mu mesons with whom I could discuss the work. In this I was more successful than I had bargained for. One of the first people I ran into was Valentine Telegdi — then of the University of Chicago, now in Zürich — whom Murph Goldberger used to refer to as Mr. Muon. Telegdi, who is of Hungarian origin, is an accomplished linguist and has a brilliant, acerbic wit. To a student who once came to him after working with another professor, he remarked, "You are a ship leaving a sinking rat." He and I had always gotten along amiably in our few encounters, so I eagerly showed him the draft of the paper. I was stunned when he said that he had seen work very much like ours. It had been done by

Henry Primakoff, a well-known theoretical physicist at Washington University. If Telegdi was the Mr. Muon of experimental physics, Primakoff was certainly the Mr. Muon of theoretical physics.

There is nothing worse than finding out that a problem you've been working on, a good problem at that, has been tackled by someone else. I did not know Primakoff at the time, but I knew that he was a first-rate scientist and a man to be taken seriously. With a heavy heart I returned to Princeton to break the news to my two senior colleagues. They were also dumfounded. They had been receiving manuscripts almost by the dozen, on a daily basis, from all over the world on the general subject of mu meson physics, and they had never seen anything on the hyperfine effect by Primakoff. They then began a literature search to see whether, by chance, he might have published something that they had missed. The search turned up nothing. At this point, they had done all that was required by the ethics of our profession. It is not necessary, or even possible, to take into account everything that someone may have written down in a private notebook.

Part of being a professional physicist is having the courage to publish your work. But Lee and Yang went beyond the conventional ethics — just as they had done with me. They called Primakoff and asked him whether he had worked on our problem. He said that he had, and that he was in the process of putting together a long manuscript — it was nearly done — and would be pleased to send us a copy of his handwritten draft. It arrived a few days later in a gigantic manila envelope. (In later years I became familiar with Primakoff's handwritten manuscripts when we worked on following up some of the details of this problem. He had an unusually ornate script, and the equations were so festooned with symbols that they looked like something out of a medieval illuminated manuscript. At one point Primakoff said to me wistfully, in his slight Southern accent, "I do not belong in this century.") When we read the manuscript, we saw that he had done things we had not done, and that we had done things he had not done. The obvious course was to publish the preliminary version jointly as a brief communication, after which Primakoff and I could continue the work. This was agreeable to everyone, and the paper came out as "The Effect of the Hyperfine Splitting of a Mu-Mesic Atom on Its Lifetime," by J. Bernstein, T. D. Lee, C. N. Yang, the Institute for Advanced Study, Princeton, New Jersey, and H. Primakoff, Washington University, St. Louis, Missouri." Here the lack of alphabetical order had nothing to do with different degrees of credit but with two groups of people working independently. Telegdi, in his inimitable way, always referred to our work as the BLYP effect — pronounced "blip" — and his group at Chicago was one of the first to measure it.

Whatever else my paper with Lee, Yang, and Primakoff did, it solved the colloquium problem. By the time I got to the Institute, the weekly "confessionals" had disappeared, although from time to time Oppenheimer would ask one of us into his office to discuss what we had been doing. On one occasion when Oppenheimer asked me, I told him the bare truth: I had been reading Proust's *Remembrance of Things Past*. I had been working very hard and was tired and had taken off a couple of weeks to read Proust. I didn't feel like making up a story. Oppenheimer gave me a kindly look and told me that when he had been about my age he had taken a bicycle trip around the island of Corsica, and that in his rucksack he had carried Proust. He read by flashlight at night while camping.

Still, it was more or less expected that everyone would give a colloquium, or part of a colloquium, during his stay. The experience could be traumatic because of Oppenheimer's often maddening behavior. He smoked incessantly — the habit finally killed him — and emitted, from time to time, a racking cough. He often interrupted the speaker with a Delphic remark, after which he would look around, I guess to see whether the others had gotten the point. He could also be brutal. Someone told me that at a seminar at Berkeley, when a pneumatic drill was being used outside the window, he interrupted the speaker to say "How can I follow this with all that noise out there, especially when that noise is making more sense than you are?" The only time he ever went after me, I thoroughly deserved it. I had asked an idiotic question about mu mesons in astrophysics, and Oppenheimer said, in a scornful tone, "Mu mesons are found at the University of Chicago and not in the stars." At this point Cohen, who was sitting next to me, whispered, "Bernstein, this is a good day to keep down in the trenches with the rest of the troops." I kept my mouth shut for the rest of the seminar.

For most of the year I had avoided giving a colloquium on the sound grounds that I didn't have anything to talk about. Now there was something to talk about, and, furthermore, Niels Bohr was visiting. Bohr, the great Danish physicist who had had a major role in establishing the quantum theory, had been in Princeton at least since New Year's Eve, a date I had very good reason to remember. Murph Goldberger and his wife, Mildred, had rented the Princeton firehouse for an enormous New Year's Eve party. They knew I played the trumpet, and Murph asked me to top off the proceedings with a rendition of "Auld Lang Syne" at midnight. When midnight arrived, I had had more than my share of the punch, but I gamely started on a pretty broken version of the melody, much to the general amusement. Just then the Oppenheimers and Bohrs walked in. Oppie listened for a minute and then gave me a very fishy look. Bohr looked amiably bemused. I decided that playing the trumpet at parties might not be what Oppenheimer had in mind for young physicists, and I didn't try it again until I left Princeton.

Soon after New Year's, Lee and Yang, in another act of generosity, invited me to present our work at a colloquium in which several of us were to tell Bohr and the rest of the group what we had been doing. I recall giving my relatively brief speech in a daze. Bohr made a few comments that were nearly incomprehensible because of his way of mumbling in all languages. I also remember that Oppie made some cryptic remarks that were inscrutable because they were inscrutable. Oppie had a way of sprinkling his conversation with obscure — at least obscure to *me* — references to the most esoteric of subjects. Many years after I left the Institute I had a chance to turn the tables. Oppenheimer had come to New York to give a lecture entitled "The Added Cubit." Before delivering the lecture, he had visited Columbia University and had challenged my colleagues there to cite the reference. No one could, and he had to tell them. News travels fast in our profession, and by afternoon someone had told me the story over the phone and given me the correct citation. By a piece of blind luck I ran into Oppenheimer in the lobby of the Algonquin Hotel later that afternoon.

The first thing he said to me was, "You're the son of a rabbi. Where does 'one cubit the more' come from?" Saying nothing about my patrimony's involving the other Testament, I answered without hesitation, "Either Matthew 6:27 or Luke 12:25: 'Is there a man among you who by anxious thought can add one cubit the more to his height?'" Oppie looked at me suspiciously and changed the subject. I never explained.

The most practical consequence of my collaboration with Lee and Yang is that I was offered a second year at the Institute. I recently came across the letter from Oppenheimer, dated February 21, 1958:

> Dear Dr. Bernstein:
>
> With the concurrence of the Faculty in Physics, I am pleased formally to offer you an extension of your membership in the School of Mathematics of the Institute for Advanced Study through the academic year 1958–1959. We can make available to you a grant-in-aid of $4,500 to defray the expenses of your extended sojourn in Princeton.
>
> We all look forward with pleasure to having you with us for a continued visit.

As you can imagine, I was extremely relieved and happy to get this letter. I had no other job, and even if I had, I would have stayed at Princeton. The stipend was identical with what I had been given the first year and in each case represented the largest sum I had ever earned. The rent on my apartment came to sixty dollars a month. There was, to be sure, an unworldly atmosphere about the Institute. . . . Though every prospect pleases. I rarely read the newspapers. In fact, I recall that one night in October of my first year, when I heard that everyone was going out to the lawn in back of the main building to watch something called Sputnik, I had no idea what it was.

Not long after my reappointment the draft board reappeared. Recently I turned up a copy of a second letter Oppenheimer wrote to them, dated April 8, 1958. It says, in part:

> We have invited Dr. Bernstein to spend another year at the Institute for Advanced Study. The work he has done here during the academic year 1957–1958 has more than fulfilled our expectations. Everything I said in my letter of last year still applies, and we very much hope that it will be possible for Dr. Bernstein to continue his work in Physics uninterrupted.

It gives me a nice feeling to think of Oppie writing those kind words so many years ago. Once again I was excused from army service. I think that this was the last time I ever heard from the board. After all, I was approaching thirty.

Now that my future had been settled for another year, I had to figure out what to do for the summer. The Institute term finished in May, and almost everyone promptly cleared out of Princeton. Cohen had been consulting during summers at the Rand Corporation in Santa Monica and was able to persuade Rand to hire me as well. The going consulting rate was forty-five dollars a day — for me, a stupendous amount of money. My Los Alamos Q clearance was still active, and so it was that in early summer I found myself in Santa Monica, by the Pacific Ocean. My own memories of that summer are absolutely vivid, just like the memory of the woman in the blockhouse that held the bombs. But in trying to check them with some of the people I recall as being present, I have discovered a kind of collective amnesia. Cohen was there and we have gone over the parts where he was involved. But for the rest — I can only set down what I remember.

In *Doctor Strangelove*, Stanley Kubrick referred to an institution with a remarkable resemblance to the Rand Corporation as the Bland Corporation. I have no idea whether he ever visited the place, but I can understand how, viewing it from the outside, he might have gotten that idea. It was then a two-story stucco building on Main Street in Santa Monica, literally within a stone's throw of the beach. The company had been founded some years earlier as an offshoot of the Douglas Aircraft Company ("Rand" was an acronym for Research and Development); I think some of the aircraft engineers at Douglas wanted a separate entity where they could work on their ideas. For that reason it had a close connection to the air force. Rand's primary function at the time I was there was to provide the theoretical underpinning for strategic air defense, which included the most effective ways for the air force to use atomic bombs if it was called on to retaliate. The place had much of the atmosphere of a small college campus, except that there were no students. But there were, for example, Russian experts who were employed to select targets in the Soviet Union whose destruction would cause the maximum damage to the country. There was a symphony orchestra made up of people who worked at Rand. There were some tennis classes, one of which I taught, along with Admiral Chester Nimitz's daughter Nancy. This was, after all, Southern California. There was also a collection of beautiful suntanned, long-legged California girls employed as secretaries. Cohen and I fell in love, usually from a safe distance, with new girls every week.

The physics division was a kind of inner sanctum. To get into it, you had to check in with a guard, who compared the photograph on your pass against your actual physiognomy each time you approached the heavy door. The division had a considerable number of comfortable offices, two of which were occupied by Cohen and me. From my office I could see the parking lot and several waving palm trees, but not the ocean. There were continual checks by people patrolling the offices to make sure that classified documents were not on the loose. Almost at once, I found the atmosphere stifling and depressing. Even Los Alamos had been nothing like this. Contributing to my sense of gloom was the Falstaffian figure of Herman Kahn. He and Cohen were great pals. Cohen informed me that on one notable occasion he had beaten Kahn in an eating contest in the Scandia Restaurant on Sunset Strip, where the smorgasbord was actually brought to the table. Cohen took advantage of Kahn's compulsive talkativeness and continued to eat while Kahn rattled on. At one crucial point Cohen managed to pull away definitively by asking Kahn a question about the strategic importance of bomb shelters. He was able to demolish a platter of smoked fish during Kahn's lengthy reply. Kahn was then, as he was to do for most of his career, "thinking about the unthinkable" — what would actually happen in a nuclear war. How many mega-deaths and all the rest. *Thinking About the Unthinkable* appeared as a book in 1962, but in 1958 he had draft chapters, which he gave various people to read and comment on. I was one of them. I refrained from making the only comment I had. The whole idea seemed to me appalling and absurd. Here we all were on this beach in Southern California — with palm trees waving outside the windows and beautiful girls inside — thinking about mega-deaths. I had no stomach for the task and gave Herman his manuscript, thanking him for letting me see it. When he asked whether I had any comments and I said no, he dismissed me as useless.

No one had any real work for me to do. That didn't matter much, since I had brought with me some of the calculations on mu mesons that I had started at Princeton. Several times a day Cohen and I would visit in his office or mine. It was a good life while it lasted, but it came to an abrupt end when a panel of distinguished physicists appeared on what I gathered was an urgent mission. I saw all of this in much the same way that the shrews must have seen the dinosaurs — from a remote niche — and have been trying, with mixed success, to put together what happened.

In October 1957 a physicist named N. C. Christofilos — one of the Livermore people — got the notion that a hydrogen bomb exploded in the magnetosphere (above the atmosphere) would produce large numbers of electrons. If enough of these bombs were exploded — *thousands* a year, he reasoned — they would produce a shield of particles that would destroy incoming enemy missiles. (I think of this as an antediluvian form of Star Wars — not that the present version makes any sense, either.) These explosions would also reproduce geophysical effects like the aurora. We could have all the auroras we wanted — any time we wanted — simply by setting off hydrogen bombs in the upper atmosphere. It sounds crazy now, but it was taken seriously at the time, and a series of three tests was planned in the South Atlantic for the summer and fall of 1958, under the rubric Argus.

In May of that year J. C. Van Allen interpreted readings from a Geiger counter installed on the first American satellite to mean that there were huge zones of charged particles — radiation belts — already trapped in the upper atmosphere. My recollection is that after the discovery of the Van Allen belts, and before the Argus tests, some astronomers, like Bernard Lovell, began objecting to the tests on the grounds that they might produce new radiation belts and thereby interfere with the natural radiation belts Van Allen had just discovered. I don't think that the main concern was fallout; that came later. There is no question, though, that a few years afterward Lovell was making a vigorous public outcry against the tests.

In any event, the physicists had arrived at Rand to show that the Van Allen belts would not be perturbed by the tests. There was a great scurrying around and at some point I was given several columns of figures to add up on a Marchant calculator. I didn't take part in the discussions of how these figures were arrived at, but I am quite sure they had to do with the possibility of deleterious effects on the upper atmosphere of the Argus tests and their successors; that is, they were meant to refute the warnings, to show that the concern being expressed was misplaced. I spent a day or two adding up these figures, then went back to my mu mesons and more or less forgot about the whole thing.

I tell this story because it had two echoes. I heard the first one in the fall of 1960, by which time I had another temporary job, at the Brookhaven National Laboratory on Long Island. Since I didn't need it, my Q clearance was no longer active. However, one afternoon I received a call from the security people, saying that a classified package had arrived for me from Rand and requesting my permission to open it. I said that I could not give my permission unless I knew what was in the pack-

age. They said they could not tell me because it was classified. I told them that was their problem. They then
phoned Rand. It turned out to be a classified report, having to do with the upper atmospheric tests, of which I was
one of several authors. That much they could tell me, but
no more, because my clearance was no longer active. The
package was sent back, unopened, to Rand, and I never
saw the report. It would be interesting to see it now, since
I think it was almost entirely wrong.

The results of the Argus tests were at first classified
but were made public in April 1959. I have taken this
chronology from an unclassified 1976 Los Alamos report
entitled "United States High-Altitude Test Experiences,"
by the late Herman Hoerlin. Dr. Hoerlin, whom I met in
the summer of 1957 in Los Alamos, began his career in
the 1930s as a cosmic ray physicist. Since the laboratories
then were at high altitudes, his vocation gave him the
chance to practice his avocation, mountain climbing. He
was one of the best climbers in the world. The Argus tests
involved small bombs launched from the deck of a ship.
"Small" means that their yield was in the range of about
a thousand tons of TNT as compared with the Hiroshima
bomb, which was 13,000 tons. They exploded at an alti-
tude of between 200 and 500 kilometers above the sea.
The earth has a magnetic field, with the north pole near,
but not at, the geographic north pole. This magnetic field
produces field lines, and trapped electrically charged particles move in helixlike orbits centered around the field
lines. In a bomb explosion, massive electrically charged
fission fragments are produced and decay into electrons
and other particles. The electrons get trapped in the field
lines and spiral until they reach the point where the lines
converge. They are then reflected back and continue to

spiral back and forth between the mirror points, meanwhile generally drifting to the east. The result is the formation of an artificial Van Allen belt; in the case of the Argus tests, belts like this were between 90 and 150 kilometers wide. Such belts are not stable, because the electrons collide with other particles and become untrapped. In the Argus tests, as Van Allen himself discovered, the artificial belts lasted only a few weeks after the explosions. However, the next test, the Starfish, was another matter.

The Starfish test, which took place on July 9, 1962, 400 kilometers above Johnston Island, involved a full-scale hydrogen bomb. It had a yield of 1.4 *million* tons of TNT. The effects of this test were completely underestimated by everyone, presumably including the authors of the report of which I was a co-author. Since I have never seen the report, I do not know what mistakes were made, and no one I have written to — the people who I thought were my co-authors — has any recollection of such a report. There the matter rests. The Starfish explosion produced an artificial Van Allen belt that lasted for years. The satellite Ariel, which was 7000 kilometers from Johnston Island four days after the explosion, operated, in Hoerlin's words, "only intermittently as a result of the deterioration of the solar cells owing to the effects of the artificial radiation belts." Two other satellites soon stopped transmitting altogether. Hoerlin estimated that an astronaut in a Skylab-type orbit one week after Starfish would have received fifty rads of radiation *per orbit.* Hoerlin pointed out that the *yearly* recommended maximum dose of radiation to the eyes is twenty-seven rads. To the best of my knowledge no one who was in the business of estimating what a test like this would produce came close to suggesting numbers of this order of magnitude. In fact, to this day, probably no one knows precisely what happened. Starfish, quite rightly, caused absolute outrage in people like Lovell. In May of 1962, prior to Starfish, he had delivered an address to the British Institute for Strategic Studies, imploring the superpowers to use the utmost caution in conducting such tests. He was ignored. After Starfish, he added a note in the printed version of his address:

> The address was delivered to the Institute of Strategic Studies nearly four months ago. In this time there have been further space activities which underline the anxiety expressed in the last paragraph of my address. . . . The United States exploded the megaton bomb outside the atmosphere and have thereby enormously confused the study of the natural radiation belts by setting up a new, long-duration zone of trapped particles. A few more explosions of this type for military purposes by other of the powers . . . will obviously add so much artificially trapped material to the radiation zones that the investigation of the natural effects will have to be abandoned before we know their true nature or origin. . . . The need for international agreement about the use of space and the control of launchings, either of rockets or space vehicles into it, has become a matter of utmost urgency.

In 1963 we signed the aboveground test ban treaty with the Soviet Union, and the tests were stopped, at least by us. The French and Chinese are still testing. It is fair to say, and Hoerlin pointed this out in his report, that the Starfish did not do lasting damage to the upper atmosphere. But that was *one* bomb. Hoerlin concluded, in his understated way, "It is also evident that the consequences of *massive* military operations in the upper atmosphere would be grave." I mention this because, although I have not worked on a classified project for over twenty years and do not have direct access to the classified aspects of Star Wars, I believe that part of the program is an attempt to revive the old idea of using artificially created Van Allen belts to stop missiles. As far as I know, the physics of this was not understood then, and I have no reason to believe that it is understood much better now.

By the time of the Starfish test I was pretty disillusioned with the "adult" world of nuclear weapons. I now knew that Adlai Stevenson had been right all along: there was no conceivable reason to test in the atmosphere and very little reason to test at all. I was also struck by the one-dimensional character of most of the people I had encountered who, in peacetime, had chosen to make their careers in nuclear weaponry. Many of these people, such as Edward Teller and Herman Kahn, were brilliant — brilliant and obsessed. They seemed to have lost touch with reality. It is a quality I see now in the new, young generation of Star Warriors. They are caught up in a new world of technology, which has become for them an end in itself — a substitution for real thought. When I hear them talk, I am reminded of myself at their age. I wonder what they will think of what they are doing when they are as old as I am now.

Back to the events of the summer of 1958. I wanted to leave Rand, but where to go? I had heard a vague rumor that Freeman Dyson was "building" a spaceship in La Jolla, south of Los Angeles, at the General Atomic Company, a recently formed private company specializing in the construction of such things as reactors. At the Institute, Dyson pretty much kept to himself. I knew him then only slightly, having asked him for some help on a physics problem that spring. It looked for a while as though electrons and positrons were behaving in an asymmetric way in certain of the weak interactions. Some papers had been written to account for this theoretically, but I thought they violated the theory of relativity, which would have been a very serious matter. I wanted to put my question in a quantitative form but had gotten stuck in the calculation.

After lunch one day I knocked on the door of Dyson's office. When I went in, I found him lounging on the brightly colored canvas beach chair that he kept for naps, reading the Bible in Russian. He explained to me that he was teaching himself Russian; since the Bible was familiar to him, it was the ideal means for learning the language. I told him my problem. He said he was a bit rusty on the kind of calculation I had in mind — it involved some of the techniques he had helped invent — but that he would have a look. We went to the blackboard, and in short order he helped me to sort things out.

I had also visited him at his house a few times, but I didn't really know him very well. While I was at Rand, however, I received a letter from the secretary we shared at the Institute, mentioning that Dyson was in La Jolla and that he had gone to Tijuana to see a bullfight and had been bitten by a dog. I wrote to him, saying that if any one of those three things was true, he was having a better time than I was. A day or two later the phone rang. It was Dyson. He suggested that I decamp from Los Angeles and come to La Jolla and join the Orion project, designing a nuclear-bomb-powered spaceship.

In *Disturbing the Universe* Dyson has given an account of this work and of his ultimate disillusionment with the idea for environmental reasons. (The version that I liked was one in which the ship was to be propelled by chemical fuels until it cleared the atmosphere, after which the bomb propulsion system would be used.) The only thing I have to add is that, characteristically, he understated his own role. He was, and still is, deeply committed to the idea of space travel, and he put every ounce of his energy and extraordinary abilities into making the design work. He did every kind of physics and engineering. It was an extraordinary *tour de force*, but as far as I know, all that effort has disappeared in a mound of classified reports.

I spent the rest of the summer working with him on "opacity" calculations — calculations involving the absorption by matter of radiation. We wanted to get out numbers, not merely formulae, and once again I found myself behind a Marchant desk calculator, adding up columns of figures. One Saturday I was in my office, adding, when Dyson came in. He noticed that I was using only three significant figures, that is, three decimal places, and he said we needed four. Then he told me that once he had done a calculation with one decimal place too few, figuring that the errors would not pile up, and at the end of the calculation had discovered that the answer was 100 percent wrong. After that homily, we started over, with his reading the numbers to four places from a table while I computed. In the end we wrote a couple of reports, which have disappeared with the rest of the project.

In September I was back in Princeton. Many of my friends and acquaintances had left. Cohen had gone to Pennsylvania. T. D. Lee had gone back to Columbia. The Feldverein had gone back to Germany and Switzerland. There were new faces, of course, but the place didn't have the same electricity it had had that first year. How could it? I am not sure whether the Institute has ever had, before or since, such a collection of physicists at just the right moment in the development of the field as was there the year of 1957–1958. Oppenheimer was right. We *had* had a ball.

I had always wanted to live in France and by late in the fall had decided to try to bring that about. I applied for a two-year National Science Foundation Fellowship to start the following September. Sputnik had frightened the government into doing something about supporting science in this country, and funds for fellowships became accessible. The one I was awarded allowed me to work on physics for two years anywhere in the world. I chose Paris . . . and a new chapter in my life. On my last day at the Institute I said goodbye to everyone; Oppenheimer wished me well. Just as I was about to leave, George Kennan came into the parking lot. He saw my packed car and asked where I was going. Paris, I said. "You will like it there," he replied.

6

The Cité

ON SATURDAY, September 12, 1959, the liner *Liberté*, under the direction of Commandant Georges Croisile, sailed from New York for Le Havre, a seven-day cruise. It was known among some of its passengers as the Fulbright Cruise, because so many of those on board were young Fulbright Scholars going to Europe for a year or two.

In addition to my two-year National Science Fellowship, I had a job; not a permanent job, but the most job-like job I had ever been offered. I was going to be a scientific associate — a junior scientist — with the theory group at the Brookhaven National Laboratory in Upton, Long Island, a laboratory largely devoted to the kind of high-energy physics I was interested in. It was not the kind of job offer to dismiss, and I had been able to work out an arrangement with the laboratory that would give me a full year abroad, followed by a stint at the laboratory, followed by another year abroad — an ideal arrangement. That the job lacked tenure was of no importance to me. I was traveling light, with no one to support, and so far each of my jobs had been on a year-to-year basis. This one actually had a two-year contract.

Before my appointment to a second year at the Institute, Oppenheimer had recommended me for another position abroad. I would have been the assistant to Wolfgang Pauli, one of the architects of the quantum theory, who taught and worked at the Eidgenössische Technische Hochschule in Zürich, Einstein's alma mater. Pauli was a true original — identical with his own caricature, as Oppenheimer once remarked. Judging from photographs, he had been reasonably well formed as a young man — quite a dancer, according to Oppenheimer. When I encountered him he was in his early fifties and was pear-shaped, with a massive head that shook back and forth or up and down, at various frequencies, depending on whether he disagreed or agreed with the speaker. He had won a Nobel Prize in 1945 — rather late, considering the magnitude of his contributions to physics — for the so-called exclusion principle, which relates to the statistics of particles like the electron and is the basis for the quantum mechanical explanation of the periodic table of elements.

Pauli had an acerbic wit and utter contempt for shoddy work in physics; his comments could be withering. He had had many postdoctoral students and assistants over the years, and I knew several of them. Victor Weisskopf had been an early Pauli assistant and sometimes told us Pauli stories at the Wednesday theoretical lunches with Schwinger in Cambridge. Two of the more recent Pauli students I knew were Roy Glauber, now a professor at Harvard, and Joaquin Luttinger, now at Columbia. Luttinger told me that Pauli once came into his office in Zürich and accused him of having done no work in several weeks. This touched a nerve, and Luttinger responded, much to Pauli's astonishment, that Pauli had not done any work in several years. Pauli went away and returned with a stack of publications to show Luttinger what, in fact, he had done. Glauber's experience with

Pauli illustrated another side of his character. He loved to tease and, having found a suitable victim, could be merciless. When Glauber was in Zürich, he made the mistake of not writing often enough to his mother, who wrote to Pauli to complain. Glauber was never allowed to forget this. Whenever Pauli saw Glauber, he would say, "And how is your dear mother?" During my tenure at the cyclotron, Pauli came to Cambridge for a visit, and Glauber and Weisskopf went to the railroad station to meet him. Weisskopf took him home, and Glauber came back to Harvard to report, with relief, that at last Pauli had forgotten about his mother; he had said nothing. What he did not know is that the minute he was out of earshot, Pauli had said to Weisskopf, "This time I will fool Glauber. I will say nothing about his mother." Pauli gave nicknames to people. My colleague Feza Gursey, who had been at Brookhaven, became known as the Brookhaven Turk. I was known as the Whisperer, because I once delivered a message to Pauli from Schwinger.

Apart from the question of Pauli's personality, which I might or might not have been able to deal with, there was the more important question of his physics. Pauli had been engaged in a peculiar enterprise with his former collaborator Werner Heisenberg, another of the great architects of the quantum theory. For a while they claimed to have solved all the unsolved problems in elementary particle theory; they reduced everything to a single equation. When calmer spirits examined the matter, they concluded that the whole thing was a chimera. The dénouement, for Pauli, came at a lecture he delivered early in 1958 at Columbia University in the large lecture hall in Pupin Laboratory. Even though there had been an attempt to keep the talk secret, the room was filled to capacity. The audience was studded with past, present, and future Nobel Prize winners, including Niels Bohr. After Pauli delivered his lecture, Bohr was asked to comment. There then occurred one of the most unusual, and in its unearthly way most moving, demonstrations I have ever witnessed. Bohr's basic point was that as a fundamental theory it was crazy, but not crazy enough. This was a very important observation. The great advances, like relativity and the quantum theory, do seem — at first sight, and especially if one has been brought up in the physics that preceded them — to be crazy, to violate common sense in a fundamental way. On the other hand, Pauli's theory was just bizarre, a strange-looking equation that stared at you like a hiero-glyph. Pauli objected to Bohr's assessment; he said the theory *was* crazy enough.

At this point these two monumental figures in modern physics began moving in a conjoined circular orbit around the long lecture table. Whenever Bohr faced the audience from the front of the table, he repeated that the theory was not crazy enough, and whenever Pauli faced the group, he would say it was. I recall wondering what anyone from the other world — the nonphysicists' world — would make of this. Dyson was asked to comment and refused. Afterward he remarked to me that it was like watching the "death of a noble animal." He was prescient. Pauli died not many months later, in 1958, at the age of fifty-eight, of a previously undetected cancer. Before that, he had renounced "Heisenberg's theory," as he now referred to it, in the most acidulous manner. One could only wonder whether Pauli's brief love affair with it was a sign that he was already ill. With Pauli's death the tradition of the Pauli assistants also died.

On the application for my fellowship, I had had to put down the place where I intended to go. I put down the École Polytechnique, the military engineering school in Paris founded by Napoleon. I cannot claim that my decision was influenced by a knowledge of either the French language or culture. I had not yet taken a single lesson in French. I was also not particularly influenced by physics. When I decided to go to Paris, French physics was barely recovering from the war. My choice had to do with some romantic idea I had about the French, acquired largely by seeing films and reading the articles about eating in France written in *The New Yorker* by the late A. J. Liebling. I was also fortunate to have become friendly with a French physicist, Louis Michel, who was a frequent visitor to Princeton while I was there.

Michel was, I thought in my ignorance, the quintessential Frenchman. He was funny both intentionally and unintentionally, the latter because of the entirely idiosyncratic way in which he spoke English. He was also an excellent physicist. Like many French university professors at that time, to make ends meet he held two jobs, one at the École Polytechnique and the other in a provincial university that he visited a few times a week. Michel was himself a graduate of the Polytechnique. After graduation the cadets are able to choose, according to their class standings, certain services to which, as I understand it, they are attached for life. The most sought-after of these was, for some reason, the Mines and the Ponts et Chausées — Bridges and Highways. Michel had ended up in the Poudre — the Gunpowder — and, in fact, had done some high-powered mathematical calculations for the Powder.

Michel is a mathematical physicist, a theoretical physicist whose strength is in the application of very advanced mathematical techniques to physics problems. When I first met him he had achieved a reputation among physicists at large for something known as the Michel parameter. This was a number that characterized the properties of the decay of the heavy electron, the so-called mu meson. Michel had done a remarkable calculation showing that this number was characteristic of the theory of the decay. The number had already been measured several times before my meeting Michel, and those measurements were in disagreement with the theory that was now emerging. The remarkable thing was that as the other experiments on other decays began to confirm the theory, the experiments on the mu decay miraculously began to confirm the theory as well, something that gives you pause when you consider the relationship between theory and experiment. Michel was in Princeton when an experimental result was announced that was exactly what was wanted. I went into his office to congratulate him. He said, "It is a pity." I asked why. "Because," he answered, "now they will speak of it no more." He was right. Once the experiment agreed with the theory, everyone lost interest in it. In any event, Michel was perfectly happy to have me put him down on my application as my destination. So it was that I found myself on the *Liberté* on my way to Paris. But, in the meanwhile, there had been a piece of serendipitous good luck involving Murray Gell-Mann.

Gell-Mann and I had been at Columbia Grammar School at about the same time, and though we are the same age — I am actually three months younger — Gell-Mann had graduated at age fourteen and gone on to Yale. From there he went to MIT, where he had gotten his Ph.D. in 1951, the year I graduated from Harvard. Odd as it may seem now, his extraordinary abilities were not widely recognized at first. He was turned down by the Princeton Graduate School and then, after his degree from MIT, was not chosen by Harvard as a Junior Fellow. He did, however, get accepted for postdoctoral work at the Institute for Advanced Study, where he was assigned an office with Francis Low. The two began a series of collaborations that had spectacular results. In 1952 Gell-Mann went to the University of Chicago, and it was here that he started producing the work that convinced everyone that a new physics superstar had arrived.

I had barely known him at Columbia Grammar and had forgotten we had any connection until he arrived at Harvard, in 1954, to give a lecture on his new work. To explain the impact that this lecture had on me I will describe very briefly the way the field of elementary particles was understood at the time. There was the work on the "conventional" elementary particles — such as the electron, the neutron, the proton, and even the pi meson — which proceeded along the lines laid down by Schwinger, Feynman, and Dyson. (Schwinger, Feynman, and Sintiro Tomanaga shared the Nobel Prize in Physics for 1965 for this work.) This is the kind of conventional theory I had been using in my thesis. But while this work was going on, a completely unexpected set of elementary particles began appearing in cosmic rays. It was not clear then, and it is not clear now, why nature has endowed us with this second layer of material reality, which, on its face, has so little to do with the material that makes up tables, apples, overcoats, you, and me. But there it is. A few new particles might not have been difficult to digest, but they kept appearing on what seemed like a weekly basis. Enrico Fermi remarked that it was getting to be like botany, and Oppenheimer proposed that a prize be given to an experimenter who did *not* find a new particle. I decided to ignore the whole thing, thinking it might go away.

Gell-Mann, at the University of Chicago, began to see how everything might fit together, how it all might be classified. This is not to explain why the new particles are there, but rather how they could be organized. This was an extremely important step. It turned noise into language. He invented what is called the "strangeness" classification. (A similar idea was created independently by T. Nakano and K. Nishijima in Japan. Part of Gell-Mann's skill is his knack for finding apt names, so his names "strangeness," "quark," and many others have become part of our language.) Strangeness is something like electric charge. It is one of the properties that characterize an elementary particle. But unlike electric charge, it is not strictly conserved in all reactions. In the strong reactions in which particles are created, it is conserved, but when these same particles decay, it can be violated, though only weakly. There are rules that govern how strangeness conservation breaks down in the decays of elementary particles. Gell-Mann published these rules in 1953. I paid little or no attention to his work. Then came his lecture.

He is a superb lecturer, and this was a bravura performance. When I first saw him, something rang a bell, and later my old yearbooks verified that this was indeed the Gell-Mann with whom our Columbia Grammar mathematics teacher Mr. Reynolds used to compare us unfavorably. His lecture convinced me that I had better wake up and begin learning about the new particles. After the revolution brought about by the work of Lee and Yang, most elementary particle theorists began to turn their attention to the theory of radioactive decays. Feynman and Gell-Mann wrote a basic paper, which was followed by a paper of Gell-Mann's that I found particularly exciting. In it he proposed a connection between electromagnetism and the weak interactions causing the decays. Not only was this a testable connection, but it suggested a variety of tests, not all of which, fortunately, Gell-Mann had worked out in his original paper. That left something for the rest of us to do. I had a like-minded colleague at the Institute, Robert R. Lewis, now of the University of Michigan, and the two of us set to work in the spring of 1958 to make a systematic study of all the reactions in which Gell-Mann's idea could be tested. We spent many days poring over tables of nuclear levels and calculating different possible measurements. We then wrote a paper on what we had found; Gell-Mann read it and responded with an amiable note.

The next fall he came to Princeton. He asked me what I was doing next year, and I told him I was going to Paris. "That's interesting," he said; "so am I." He had been invited by several French institutions and was going as the joint guest of the Sorbonne and the Collège de France. He suggested we might work together and added, "Stick with me, kid, and I'll put you on Broadway." Wherever Gell-Mann was, I knew, there was certain to be one of the centers of activity in the theory of elementary particles — a wonderful chance for me.

The summer before my trip to France, I had been in La Jolla, once again working with Freeman Dyson on the Orion spaceship. Apart from the experience, the job had given me a little extra money, which I used to buy a car that was to be delivered to the boat on its arrival in Le Havre. I also used some of my Orion money to try to learn French. I had read Proust in English and seen some French films with subtitles, and that was my total exposure to the language. There was, however, a Berlitz School in San Diego, and I signed up for private French lessons. My instructor was a charming and entirely serious young woman, but the situation was hopeless. I studied with her for something like three hours a week, perhaps less, for a little over a month. The conversation, such as it was, was supposed to be entirely in French: she held up cards with pictures of things like flowers while she repeated words like *coquelicot*. It was entertaining but did not advance things substantially. I finally decided that it didn't matter; I would learn all the French I needed by listening to people talk on the street. Little did I know.

Michel had promised to look into a place for me to live, but I had had no reply to the letter I wrote to him during the summer. Just when I had given up, a letter came addressed to Monsieur Jeremy BERNSTEIN, BROOKHAVEN NATIONAL LABORATORY, Department of Physics, UPTON, NEW JERSEY. The fact that Michel had placed the laboratory in the wrong state may have had something to do with the letter's delay in reaching me. It is a splendid illustration of the essential Michel:

Dear Jeremy,

Sorry not to have replied to your first letter. I am still alive, but not in Paris. Nobody is in Paris now except Americans. I will be back there around October 1rst (1959!). I am sorry not to be able to welcome you in Paris. For a place to live, I would suggest you contact:

Maison des États-Unis = American Foundation de la Cité Universitaire, 15, boulevard Jourdan-PARIS XIV. It is near to me and very convenient to go to the École Polytechnique ou Normale.

Do not forget that by January all theoretical Physics (not de Broglian) will move in Orsay, Cité Universitaire is just on the suburb line. I cannot be very helpful otherwise, before getting Paris.

Enjoy your times in September. If you need to work, use my office in the École Polytechnique, 17, rue Descartes–Paris V. Ask the porter to see Miss POUDEROUS, my secretary. She will know about it.

See you soon

Yours,

L. Michel

That was it. Much of the letter I did not understand at all. I did not know what the Cité Universitaire was, and the reference to all non–de Broglian physicists moving out of Paris in January was also a total mystery. I knew who Louis de Broglie was. He was the French nobleman who in 1923 postulated the wave nature of matter — the beginning of modern quantum theory — which became his doctoral thesis in 1924 and for which he won the Nobel Prize in 1929. He had then turned against the conventional quantum theory and had established an institute in Paris devoted to nonconventional physics, about which there were very mixed reports. That his followers were not leaving Paris was, it seemed to me, either a good or a bad thing, but in any case not especially relevant to me. What came as a shock was that Michel would not be there in September, but the die was cast, and I was on my way.

The week-long crossing went by in a delightful haze. Early in the week, when scanning the passenger list, I noticed a familiar name, Thomas Ypsilantis. I had never met Ypsilantis, but I knew he was one of the four experimental physicists who had discovered the antiproton in Berkeley in 1955. The other three were Claude Wiegand, Owen Chamberlain, and Emilio Segrè. In the mysterious ways of the Nobel committee, only Chamberlain and

Segrè were awarded the Nobel Prize for this work, in 1959. I had seen Ypsilantis at a few conferences; he seemed a cheerful, happy-go-lucky sort, someone to look up on a cruise. So I did. I found that he, too, was heading for Paris. Since I expected to have a car meeting me at the boat, I proposed that we join forces and drive there together. When the boat docked, not only was there a magnificent Hillman Minx convertible waiting for me, there was also another communication from Michel. This one announced that there was no room for me at Maison des États-Unis but that a room had been reserved for me at the Maison de Cuba, whatever that was. Ypsilantis and I packed our gear into the Hillman and drove through the magnificent early fall countryside to Paris, where we went our separate ways.

My first task was to find the Cité Universitaire and then the Maison de Cuba. The Cité is located in a large parklike area on the south side of Paris, near the Port d'Orléans. The place was dotted with pavilions representing various countries and French territories. It looked, at first, like a kind of student world's fair. It was never entirely clear to me who was actually entitled to live there and, indeed, in what sense you needed to be a student. The rules for parking your car, which I had to do before locating the Maison de Cuba, were somewhat involuted. The object of the exercise was to find a parking place near the fence on the other side of the broad sidewalk along the Boulevard Jourdan. There were a few places where a bit of a driveway gave access to the sidewalk. You then drove down the sidewalk until, with luck, you found a parking place. Later in the year this mad arrangement led me to an unexpected encounter.

One morning I was in a hurry to get somewhere. The

night before, I had found a parking place a long way from a driveway, which meant that I had to drive down the sidewalk a considerable distance. There were two large pedestrians in front of me, walking along slowly, as was their legal right. Such was my hurry that I absent-mindedly honked my horn. They turned around, furious. They were cops — *flics*. They came over in a rage. The number of things I had done wrong were countless. Driving down the sidewalk and honking at pedestrians figured significantly among them. By this time I had acquired some French and a strategy for dealing with situations like this. I remained perfectly mute and attempted to give the impression that I was, in all senses, a dumb foreigner. I could tell that the cops were either going to arrest me or give me a lecture and let me go. They decided on the lecture. I listened attentively. At the end of it, forgetting my disguise, I asked in halting but workable French whether it was illegal to park where I parked and where, indeed, I and everyone else at the Cité with a car had been parking for months. "No," said one, "it is not illegal but it is a bad habit." I thanked him politely and drove off down the sidewalk.

My first impression of the Maison de Cuba was not very favorable. It was a dark and gloomy place, and the matron who ran it matched her surroundings. I had been assigned a back room on the second floor. It was a bit like a monk's cell, with an adjoining bathroom separated from the bedroom by a cloth curtain. The contrast to my "garden apartment" at Princeton, with its designer furniture, could not have been more striking. I put away my things and then headed in the general direction of the École Polytechnique to locate Michel's secretary, Miss Pouderous.

Not long ago I walked through those familiar streets of the Latin Quarter, and it seemed to me that the heart had gone out of the place. In term time, the place used to be alive with students. Now the university is decentralized; even the Polytechnique has moved out of Paris. In 1959, when I arrived, before the start of classes, I found the area deserted. The École Polytechnique looked like a walled *caserne*, and even after several visits I had difficulty finding my way inside. Miss Pouderous turned out to be very efficient; she managed to explain to me, in a mixture of French and English, that Michel was in his country home and would not be back for at least ten days. It seemed to me that the wisest course was to get back into my car and drive south, to the Riviera. Ypsilantis had spoken favorably of a hotel in Cannes, and so it was that I spent the next ten days at the Hôtel Montmorency on the beach.

There is nothing like a week by the sea to cheer me up. When I returned to Paris, even the Cité Universitaire, with its autumn chestnut trees, had a certain romantic aura, and I set out to explore its facilities. There were the pavilions where the students — or whatever they were — actually lived. Next to the Maison de Cuba was the Maison de L'Indo-Chine, shaped like a pagoda. The American Pavilion was a rectangular brick structure with separate wings for men and women. The Maison de Cuba, happily, seemed to be entirely coeducational. There were even couples with small children living in some of the rooms. Apart from myself, the only non-Cuban there in my time was a bilingual Canadian named John Potter, who was also a physicist. Potter had an impish sense of humor and enjoyed introducing me to some of the Cuban revolutionary residents as "my American friend." He liked to see the expressions on everyone's face as this piece of information was digested. The crone who ran the place turned out to be an amiable sort, provided you didn't make waves. I was not a student and, I am sure, had no legal right to be living there, but nothing was ever said, probably because I paid the modest rent on time.

There was a communal restaurant that served edible food for very little money, along with cheap wine in half bottles with foil caps. In the beginning, before I'd picked up any French, I found the multiple and rapid conversations utterly bewildering and took to having most of my meals in the small cafés and restaurants of the *quartier*, a thoroughly bourgeois neighborhood with no tourist attractions other than the Cité itself. Next to the dining facilities were the tennis courts, such as they were, and they lead me to a tale that will require a little backtracking to relate.

Tennis had been a part of my family *gestalt* ever since I could remember. I had played some competitive tennis in high school and continued to play at Harvard, though I wasn't good enough to make any of the teams. A friend in graduate school, named Charles Hubbard, who was a first-rate tennis player told me that there were tournaments in many tennis clubs not far from Boston. He played in them regularly, and I started to go with him. The entry fees were very small, and if I got a really good player to play with, I could look at it as an inexpensive tennis lesson. At Princeton, I managed to practice with the freshman team, and when I worked with Dyson on the spaceship, I spent most of my weekends playing in small tennis tournaments in towns near San Diego. It was a great way to meet people and to see parts of the countryside I'd otherwise not have seen.

When I went to Paris I had the naïve idea that French universities, like their American counterparts, would have tennis teams and that I could continue playing. Of course, the mere idea of the Sorbonne having a tennis team was enough to send any French intellectual into paroxysms of laughter. There were, however, those tennis courts at the Cité. Not only were they in poor shape, but it was next to impossible to get to play on them. The nets seemed to be the private property of certain "students," who played among themselves and with cronies. During several weeks of trying I managed one game and then gave up. This momentary setback was to have remarkable consequences.

By now, Michel had returned to Paris, and we set up shop in the basement of one of the buildings in the Polytechnique, and it gradually became evident to me just how peculiar Michel's situation was. To put the matter in context, I think it is fair to say that he was at that time the best-known French theoretical physicist, along with Maurice Lévy, who was at the École Normale Superieure. The two men had a correct but not especially cordial relationship. It was typical that once I learned to speak French, I could *tutoyer* both men, though they formally "*vousvoyered*" each other. Despite Michel's international reputation, his actual position at the École Polytechnique was *maître de conférences* — a sort of associate professor — in the laboratory of one Jean Vignal, who was the professor. The unfortunate fact was that Vignal, a marine engineer, did not know any modern physics. He was an elderly gentleman whose education in physics seems to have stopped somewhere in the late 1920s. He taught students entirely incorrect things in the very field in which Michel was an acknowledged master. (Vignal, for example, had the idea that the electrons in beta radioactivity emerged with a single energy. It was the fact that they didn't that led Pauli, in the early 1930s, to invent the neutrino.) On top of that he often repeated lectures, which caused the students to chant, in chorus, *"Déjà vu!"*

Michel had an incendiary temperament and less than even the minimum tolerance for fools, which made his situation potentially explosive. Matters might have been smoothed over if the experimental group, led by the noted physicist Louis le Prince Ringuet, had had a serious interest in theory. Le Prince Ringuet was a colorful cosmic ray experimenter who distinguished himself at Rochester Conferences by giving bilingual lectures that sounded like performances by Maurice Chevalier. As far as Le Prince Ringuet was concerned, theoretical physics was an idle luxury. He was a true Baconian, who believed that all you had to do is to put your photographic plate somewhere and the Lord would provide. To do an experiment with something in mind was an anathema to him. Michel and Le Prince Ringuet hardly spoke to each other. Despite these tensions, Michel had managed to gather around him a small group of devoted and brilliant students, some of whom are now among the leaders of French physics.

For some time before I arrived, pressure had been building to move much of the scientific faculty out of Paris to a new, American-style campus that was being constructed at Orsay, a relatively short commute from town. The high-energy-theory group was being created by Lévy. Michel was to join it after the first of the year, and I was to move with him. But before that took place things developed along three fronts: French, tennis, and physics. The French was the key to everything else.

My plan had been to absorb French osmotically from taxi drivers, newspapers, my car radio, and waiters. This worked as long as all I wanted to do was to order simple meals in restaurants or take a taxi to the Champs-Elysées. But it soon became clearer and clearer to me that getting beyond that stage was going to be impossible without help — a lot of help. It also became clear that unless I learned the language, my time in Paris was going to be lonely and frustrating. Two things convinced me that I had better do something. The first was a little reception given by the commandant of the École Polytechnique for the faculty and visitors. I was invited to accompany Michel. The guests were evidently a distinguished group. The tradition of mathematics at the Polytechnique had always been very strong. When I was there, the great mathematician Jacques Hadamard, who was in his nineties, gave a retirement address, and Laurent Schwartz, considered to be one of the greatest mathematicians in the world, was then on the faculty. It would have been nice to talk to him and others at the reception. They were very polite and initially interested in my having come from America, but as soon as they found that I could not carry on a sensible conversation in French, they lost all interest. I left the reception feeling like a moron.

The second thing was that I had not managed to meet any girls. Paris in the fall can be one of the most romantic cities in the world, and it can also be one of the loneliest. Once the students got settled, the Latin Quarter burst into life. The cafés were full of couples engaged in what I took to be brilliant, scintillating conversation. The whole Latin Quarter, with its side streets and curious buildings bathed in the soft light of autumn, was like a bittersweet French love song. One morning I came to work early by bus. (By this time I had decided that, to keep my sanity, it was better to save my car for special occasions. On asking Michel for a hint about driving in Paris, I was told, "*Mon cher*, if you want the right of way, take it." Instead, I began taking the bus.) It was a lovely fall morning and I was in a mood that could be characterized as what the late Reinhold Niebuhr had once called "neurotic preoccupation with self" — that is, bathos. At the foot of the bus was a beautiful red-haired girl. She made my heart stop. When I got off the bus, much to my astonishment she approached me and said, "*J'ai vous aimée.*" In my bewilderment and linguistic ineptitude, I did not notice that she had used the past tense. That dawned on me later, after I had spent the equivalent of three dollars to buy the awful poetry magazine she was selling. That was it. I was going to learn to speak French.

But how? There was a bewildering variety of entities, most of which advertised in the *International Herald Tribune*, offering to teach French with varying degrees of painlessness. They ranged from private tutors to schools like Berlitz. I had no idea which to choose, so I asked Michel. On this subject he was categorical. The only place for me to go was the Alliance Française, on the Boulevard Raspail, not far from the Sorbonne. He told me that its purpose was to teach French to foreigners, that all the instruction was in French, and that the only common language most of the students had was French. "*Très sérieux*," Michel added solemnly.

I headed for the school. It consisted of a little group of buildings that included a student restaurant. The whole atmosphere had a no-nonsense sobriety about it. There were five degrees, ranging from total novice to interpreter. The evening classes I was interested in met five nights a week for something like two hours a session. I decided to enroll in the second level, since by then I had a smattering of restaurant and taxi French. I was given a student card that entitled me to eat in the terrible student restaurants in the Latin Quarter and probably legitimated my stay in the Maison de Cuba. The cost was extremely reasonable, and there was the bonus that something like half the class consisted of au pair girls from Germany, Great Britain, and Scandinavia. In short, the fat was in the fire. The only other American in my class was another physicist, Robert Tripp, a colleague of Ypsilantis's at Berkeley who was also spending a year in Paris. We engaged in fierce contests to see which of us could get the highest grades on the *dictée*, that diabolical examination in which the teacher reads a passage in French while the students copy it down. Anyone who has been subjected to this form of instruction knows the traps one can fall into with words that sound alike but have different spellings and accents. In addition to the dictée we had homework assignments, regular tests, and many hours of classroom conversation in which we got to know, to some extent, our classmates. Many were refugees, either from the East or from Franco's Spain. Learning to speak and write French correctly was for them a vital necessity. Once a week, after class, Tripp and I treated ourselves to a late meal at one of the restaurants starred in Michelin. Our ambition was to eat our way through the stars, and I still have the 1959 Michelin with the restaurants systematically crossed off. In due course, I found myself a German girlfriend from our class. She was in Paris as an au pair and had blue eyes that glowed like those of a porcelain cat. Life began to look a lot better.

If you have ever tried in adulthood to learn a foreign

language, you will probably never forget the moment when you discover that you can think in that language. What critical mass of neuronal crossings must take place for that to happen, I do not know, but it is a truly remarkable experience. It happened to me one morning a few months after I had begun my classes. I was driving somewhere with the car radio turned on, and it suddenly dawned on me that I was understanding the French directly, without making any mechanical translation in my head. It was a fantastic sensation. From that point on I immersed myself in French. There were dozens of small nightclubs in the Latin Quarter that featured singers like Jacques Brel and Ricet Barrier, who were just getting known. The one I liked the best was called the Cheval d'Or. It looked at first like a *boucherie chevaline* — a butcher shop with a horse's head in front. Inside, it was a small nightclub where the only drinks served were colas and fruit juices. The club was a jumping-off place for artists who later became famous but would return out of gratitude to the manager. It was extremely cheap and absolutely delightful — and, like so much of the Latin Quarter, it no longer exists. On Sundays I often went to the Odéon Théâtre, where Jean-Louis Barrault was staging such plays as *Rhinocéros* by Ionesco, or *Tête d'Or* by Claudel. Sometimes I went to Montmartre, to the Bobino, to hear singers and comedians who were well established — people like Léo Ferré and Georges Brassens.

Because I was living with students, my French was really argot, student slang and worse. This was to reverberate in a very peculiar way a few years later, when I began climbing with the Chamonix guides in the French Alps. In my second year of climbing I was assigned, quite accidentally, Claude Jaccoux, who over the years has become one of my closest friends. Jaccoux later told me that when he heard, on our first climb, that his client was an American, his heart sank; there would be the language barrier. He was amazed, therefore, by my reaction to the first serious difficulty: I emitted a stream of argot that would have done credit to a French sailor. He was so favorably impressed that he invited me to dinner with his family that very night.

Now that my French was evolving, my next concern was tennis. The only other form of physical exercise that was convenient was swimming — there was a pool at the Cité — but I had no intention of getting back into a pool. I looked around the Latin Quarter for tennis clubs and soon found one with a court that appeared to be surfaced with some kind of linoleum. Two men were bounding around it dressed in long white pants. The whole thing had a decadent, Proustian air, and I decided that the place was not for me, especially after I learned the price, which was astronomical. Once again I put the matter to Michel, and once again he did a very generous thing. He knew that Le Prince Ringuet had been one of the better tennis players in France. Although he was then in his fifties, he still competed in tournaments. Michel also knew that Le Prince Ringuet belonged to one of the better tennis clubs in Paris: the Tennis Club of Paris in the Bois de Boulogne. Even though he and Le Prince Ringuet were not on very good terms, he arranged for us to meet to discuss tennis. Le Prince Ringuet was extremely cordial and made a date with me to play at his club a few days later.

The place was like a vision: wonderful red clay tennis courts set among flower beds. There was an entire building filled with magnificent, verdant indoor courts. These were used, I later learned, for the French national indoor championships, which attracted top players from all over Europe. There was a first-class dining facility and gym. Every prospect did indeed please.

Le Prince Ringuet beat me in our match but had enough of a workout so that he asked whether I would like to join his club. It took a great deal of restraint to keep my acceptance of his invitation suitably modulated. I was introduced to the club secretary and returned to Paris in a state of euphoria. This was short-lived. A few days later Le Prince Ringuet had to report that there was a waiting list for membership in the tens, if not hundreds, and that I could not be accommodated by the normal route — whatever that meant. I tried not to let my disappointment show too much. He went on to say, however, that now that his honor was at stake, he would continue to pursue the matter. Some days later he gave me a delightful piece of intelligence. He had discovered that there was a second class of membership, open to non-French citizens, called a diplomatic membership. It had all the privileges of the regular membership but cost somewhat less. By pulling a few strings, he had obtained one of them for me. I could have embraced the man.

The club membership added an entirely new dimension to my life in Paris. Apart from enjoying the physical exercise, I could observe *le tout* Paris at play. Jacques Chaban Delmas, later prime minister, was one of the better players; my neighbor in the locker room was Budge Patty, a fashionable American living in Paris who was at that time ranked in the top five in the world. I recall his coming back to our locker area after he had been soundly beaten by the Dane Kurt Nielson in the French Indoor, and saying, again and again, to himself or me, "I hate it . . . I hate it." I think he quit playing in tournaments not long after.

One of the most interesting characters I encountered in the club was another American, Wayne Van Voorhees. He earned his living partly by playing tennis and partly by doing bit parts in French gangster films. His French was heavily accented, so as a rule he played Italian gangsters. This was still the time when tennis "amateurs" were being paid under the table, a horrid system. Van Voorhees told me tales about how these illegal payments were made and how they depended on how far a player got in a given tournament. Van Voorhees was not quite as good as Budge Patty, but he was in the same general league, and the two of them practiced together frequently. Van Voorhees said that after he was admitted to the club, no one would play with him for quite a while. This also happened to me, and it took me several weeks to find a congenial group of players. The idea of a club secretary arranging matches among strangers seems to be foreign to the French ethos. Van Voorhees finally got asked to play by one of the weaker members of the club, whom he promptly dispatched, six–love, six–love. He was then asked to play by stronger players, whom he similarly defeated. This went on until he had worked his way up the ladder and it became clear to everyone that, despite his unassuming and congenial appearance, he was one of the best players in the world. Van Voorhees's march through the Tennis Club of Paris is like a Walter Mitty story come true. I used to tease him that he couldn't be that good because he refused to play with me. Of course, he refused to play with me because it would have been a total waste of his time. Then, one night — we could play indoors at night — he said, "All right, I've had enough of this. Get dressed and we'll play." I got into my shorts and we had at it. My recollection is that we began about seven in the evening and quit about eleven. I think we played six sets, in which I did not win a single point. What interested me was how this came about. I thought he might simply blow me off the court — hit the ball so hard that I wouldn't be able to return it at all. But that's not what happened. Each shot that he hit was within a few inches of a line. I would run like a Scotch terrier and get it back — sometimes — and then it would be a few inches from another line. Van Voorhies was much amused.

Meanwhile, the physics was proceeding apace. Before I left the Institute, Oppenheimer had told me that he and his wife were planning to visit Paris in the fall; he had given me his address and his dates. I looked him up at the Hôtel Paris Dinard, and we had a very relaxed and pleasant visit. He had just come from seeing his friend André Malraux. I do not know whether it was before or after this visit that Malraux announced his view of what Oppenheimer should have done in his hearing before the Atomic Energy Commission. Malraux's notion was that Oppenheimer should have stood up and said, "*Je suis la bombe atomique,*" and then walked out. Malraux apparently did not know that it was Oppenheimer who requested the open hearing in order to refute charges that had been made against him by Lewis Strauss, the head of the AEC. Oppenheimer had the option of resigning as a consultant to the commission, but he chose not to do so, because he believed that his resignation would be construed as an admission of guilt. He could not leave the matter unresolved. It is easy to say in hindsight what he should have done, but I believe that nothing he might have said at the hearing would have changed the outcome, although he probably should have insisted that courtroom rules of evidence be followed instead of the improvised rules that were employed. The only time Oppenheimer ever volunteered to me anything about what he referred to as "my case," he said that all the time the matter was running its course, he felt as if it were happening to someone else. I did not know Oppenheimer before the proceedings, but those who did say that the hearings broke his heart.

Once Oppenheimer left Paris, Michel and I got down to work and produced a small paper. Recently I was amused to see that the contents of that paper, which we wrote so many years ago in the basement of the École Polytechnique, were given as a homework problem for graduate students in a standard text on elementary particle theory. Perhaps, twenty-five years from now, it will be given as a problem in a textbook for high school seniors.

I had come to Paris with a second physics problem that had been nagging at me ever since I left Princeton. It was a sort of pedagogical problem, too technical to describe here, that was connected to the theory of radioactive decays that Feynman and Gell-Mann had proposed. I explained my question to Michel, who said it sounded good enough to work on. It was by now early November, about the time that Gell-Mann had said he would be arriving in Paris. In fact, no sooner had Michel and I begun to formulate what it was that we wanted to study, and how we might go about it, than Gell-Mann himself walked into our basement. He asked us what we were doing and I explained. He said something about the problem's sounding interesting and then disappeared. The next day, at about the same hour, he reappeared and said in his perfect French, *"Messieurs, le problème est résolu."* He must have spent all night on it. What he had done was produce a general framework that could accommodate our problem along with one that he had been working on. Michel and I were stupefied. I decided that this would be a real opportunity to see how creative physics of the highest order is done — a little like playing Van Voorhees in tennis.

Unlike several of the first-rank physicists, Gell-Mann genuinely likes to collaborate. He seems to need someone to bounce ideas off. My colleague, the late John Sakurai, once asked Dirac, over dinner at the Institute, whether he had ever had a priority fight over any of his ideas. Dirac answered, succinctly, "The really good ideas are had by only one person." He almost never collaborated. Many of Gell-Mann's most outstanding papers were done by himself, and there is the one great paper with Feynman. But when it comes to working out the ramifications of ideas, Gell-Mann, more often than not, works with other people. In Paris there were basically four of us, Michel and I and Gell-Mann and Maurice Lévy. We saw each other almost daily and exchanged all kinds of ideas, and I had the chance to see whether I could figure out what made Gell-Mann tick. What was the secret of that kind of scientific creativity? I finally decided, after almost a year, that I hadn't learned the secret and that, in some sense, it could not be understood.

In a way I pity the historians of science and others who are attempting to put together a reliable history of the postwar development of elementary particle physics. At first sight the problem seems almost trivial; all you have to do, you may think, is ask the participants for their accounts of what happened. But such stories can be woefully misleading. I've been astonished to read descriptions of events I had witnessed whose meaning at the time seemed completely different from these later versions. This disparity may reflect my faulty memory — or it may reflect a not unnatural desire by the participants to make things appear more coherent than they actually were. Having issued this caveat, I will try to describe the work done by Gell-Mann in Paris that led to his creation, the following fall, of what he called the Eightfold Way and then the quark.

Gell-Mann had a particular method of working. Periodically, he summarized what he had been doing. The summaries were, in effect, manuscripts of papers, though he often did not publish them. Writing the papers was his way of collecting his thoughts. He let me read some of these handwritten manuscripts. Their theme and the theme of the work that Gell-Mann told me about when we talked together several times a week was the same — it was an attempt to find a unifying symmetry principle that would give meaning to the newly discovered strange particles. The problem was that the experiments did not suggest such a symmetry. Indeed, the events that occurred in the discovery of this principle were, as far as I am concerned, a perfect counter to Le Prince Ringuet's Baconian notion of going into the laboratory with an open mind and no theoretical guidance. If his method had been followed, no one would have gotten anywhere in the physics of elementary particles.

Since experiment was of little or no help, what took place, as far as I could make out, was a kind of theoretical "playing around." Gell-Mann had various mathematical objects and was playing with them like toys. He would say to me such things as "The currents are commuting like angular momenta." Given the currents in question, this seemed a true statement, but one whose significance was beyond me. I did not see why it was of any interest.

Occasionally he would come up with a new form of current that had even "cuter" algebraic properties, which he would be very pleased with and which meant even less to me. I am afraid I tried his patience with my obtuseness. It got to the point where I would hide out for a few days just to try to make sense of what was going on. When I called Gell-Mann, he would say, "Where have you been. I've discovered millions of things." As far as I could see, there was not the remotest hint that any of this was leading anywhere. It seemed to me like open-ended speculation, but in this I was entirely wrong. When Gell-Mann returned to Cal Tech in the fall of 1960, and began talking to a mathematician named R. Block, he came to realize that there was a name for what he was doing — generating Lie groups — and that it had been, since its invention by the Norwegian mathematician Sophus Lie at the end of the nineteenth century, a well-formulated branch of pure mathematics. Viewed this way, and in retrospect, a program of how to proceed is quite clear. You would make a systematic study of the simple Lie groups, looking for one with properties that resemble those of the elementary particles. Indeed this is how Gell-Mann did it after Block pointed out to him that these groups had been classified by the French mathematician E. Cartan. As it happened one of the most elementary Lie groups worked, although it wasn't until 1964 that a group of thirty-three physicists at the Brookhaven Laboratory found the key particle whose existence Gell-Mann had predicted, along with its essential properties. It is impossible to believe that this very odd particle — known as the omega-minus — would have been found if no one had been looking for it; and if it had been found without the theory, its existence would have seemed incomprehensible. In 1969

Gell-Mann was awarded the Nobel Prize in Physics for this work. I doubt whether there have been many more deserving recipients.

Some time after the new year Michel and I left the Polytechnique and moved out to the newly built scientific campus at Orsay. It was a modern-looking place, lacking the wonderful patina of the Latin Quarter. It was also surrounded by mud, because the grass had not yet grown. I went out there once or twice a week and otherwise worked either with Gell-Mann or by myself in Paris. Before long, Michel left Orsay. A private industrialist gave enough money so that a kind of clone of the Institute for Advanced Study could be founded in Bures-sur-Yvette, a small country town close to Orsay. It now has as members several very distinguished mathematical physicists and pure mathematicians, among them René Thom, the founder of catastrophe theory. Michel was, I think, the first physics member to be appointed, and he has been one ever since.

That spring I did some traveling — some on my own and some to give talks on the work we had been doing in Paris. Although nothing had been formally published, the grapevine in physics is very active, and it was widely known what we'd been up to. Gell-Mann was lecturing all over the place, and I got a chance to do some lecturing as well, in Vienna and, most interesting for me, at the Eidgenössiche Technische Hochschule in Zürich, where I might have gone as Pauli's assistant.

During the year, Gell-Mann, knowing of my rabbinical family background, enjoyed teasing me by taking potshots at Israel. This may have been revenge for an incident of the previous spring, when we had gone to call on Abba Eban, then Israel's ambassador in Washington.

He was an old friend of my father's, and I had arranged the visit and had taken Gell-Mann along. Eban reminisced about my family and then turned to Gell-Mann and asked, "Are you also a physicist?" Certainly he had meant no harm, but Gell-Mann was somewhat less than pleased. Now I was planning to go to Israel that coming April and was surprised to learn that Gell-Mann also expected to visit the country the same month. He had been invited to lecture at several places; furthermore, the trip would give him a chance to do some exotic bird watching. Gell-Mann has been a devoted bird watcher since childhood. Indeed, one day a few years later, while visiting him in his office at Cal Tech, I noticed a list of items requiring attention on his blackboard; one item was "hummingbirds." When I questioned him, he said that Crawford Greenewalt, the chief executive officer of the Du Pont Company and an expert on hummingbirds, had asked him whether he could explain the iridescence of the hummingbird wing. Gell-Mann had found out that it was a subtle optical effect that depended on the angles at which the bird's feathers were set. Israel happens to be a stopover for more than six hundred kinds of migratory birds, many of which Gell-Mann had never seen. Thus it was that early in April each of us headed to Israel.

I planted myself in the Hotel Migdal David in Tel Aviv, a class C hotel "for tourists with limited means," and the next day was off to the Weizmann Institute, in Rehovoth, where Gell-Mann was giving a lecture. He informed me that he had been assigned a Jeep, a driver, and an ornithologist, and that very day he was off to watch birds. He invited me to go along. I can take or leave the birds, but it seemed a pleasantly unconventional way to see the countryside, so I accepted. The driver turned out to be a tough former soldier armed with a revolver. We were planning to spend the second day of our birding at Lake Huleh, which is close to the Syrian border. The driver was taking no chances. Soon after we set out on the first day, it became clear that Gell-Mann knew as much or more about the local birds than did the local ornithologist, who then asked for an explanation of parity nonconservation. We spent that night in the city of Safed, the lovely town that for centuries has been a retreat for Jewish mystics.

The next day we were up at five to drive to Lake Huleh to see the birds. I had misgivings about Gell-Mann's running around that area, with field glasses, shouting things like "There's a roller," and waving amiably to the Syrian border guards, but nothing happened.

When we got back to Tel Aviv, I began to look up people to whom I had letters of introduction, including Ben Gurion's daughter Renanah and her husband. This led to an invitation for Gell-Mann and myself to visit Ben-Gurion, who was in his desert retreat at S'deh Boker, a kibbutz in the Negev. It was a rugged, isolated place, and the Ben Gurions were living in a simple cottage guarded by armed soldiers. The former prime minister was a small impish man with an aureole of white hair. When we were taken inside, his wife, known in Israel as the archetypal Jewish mother, began questioning us on our marital status. Gell-Mann was married, and I wasn't, and that provoked hypotheses on my family's feelings on the matter. (The Ben-Gurions had known my parents for many years.) I told Mrs. Ben-Gurion that happiness was not everything and that, anyway, I was perfectly happy without it. With that she dropped the subject.

Ben-Gurion had recently been in Washington, where

he had met President Kennedy, whom he referred to with affection as a *"yingele."* He must have been briefed about Gell-Mann, because he made a pitch for him to take a job in Israel. (Curiously, after Gell-Mann discovered the Eightfold Way the following year, he learned that the mathematics of it had been discovered independently at about the same time by a young Israeli named Yuval Née-man. It was in his Ph.D. thesis.) Ben-Gurion had a high voice and at one point all but shouted at Gell-Mann — causing some of the guards posted at the windows to look inside to see what was happening — "Do you see those trees on that hill there?" We looked; there were no trees. "Yes," he said dramatically, "but in ten years there will be!" It was a powerful display of personality, but Gell-Mann returned to Cal Tech.

By the end of April I was back in Paris. The problem of how to spend the summer had been resolved by an enticing invitation. Maurice Lévy, with whom Michel and I had been collaborating, had founded a summer school of physics on the island of Corsica. The previous summer had been its first season of operation, and he invited me to be a member of its faculty for its second year, which meant I would be giving lectures in French. I knew next to nothing about Corsica except that Corsicans were the butt of innumerable music hall jokes in Paris. (A typical one: Wife to husband: "Antoine, put on your revolver and take out the garbage.") It was supposed to be a wild but beautiful place. The school was near a beach in the village of Cargèse. The students lived in tents and the faculty in a modest but charming hotel on the beach called the Thalassa. It all sounded spectacular, and so it turned out to be.

In the fall of 1960, I returned to the United States

and to the Brookhaven National Laboratory. It was (and is) a wonderful place scientifically, but for me, after my year in France, it caused a drastic culture shock. I felt as I suppose many Americans have felt who have spent time abroad and have learned to speak another language — suspended between two worlds. I did a not very original thing: I began to write. What was mostly on my mind was France and the island of Corsica, so I wrote about them. Eventually what I wrote became a sort of love letter, which I called "Annie of Corsica." I showed it to a few people at the laboratory, including the late Samuel Goudsmit, the man who had hired me, and the Nobel Prize winner Edward Purcell, who was visiting the laboratory from Harvard. "Why not send it to *The New Yorker*?" they said. I did, and it was accepted. It was, apart from the letter I wrote as a child about the *Big Little Books*, the first professional writing I had ever done. I now had two professions — and this book is the result.

Afterword

IN A FAIRY TALE, the adult life of the young couple is usually summarized by the sentence "They lived happily ever after." As I had told Mrs. Ben-Gurion, I have never felt that the achievement of happiness was a very important goal. There is a song by Léo Ferré that says, "*Le bonheur ce n'est pas grande chose. C'est que le chagrin que s'repose.*" I can't say whether these early years of my life — the ones I have been describing — were happy or not. They were purposeful in a way that one's adult years are not. When I was interviewing Rabi for my *New Yorker* profile on him, he said, "I think physicists are the Peter Pans of the human race. They never grow up, and they keep their curiosity. Once you are sophisticated, you know too much — far too much." During my "ungrown years" I had almost no responsibilities. I had no family to support, no classes to teach, and no taxes to pay. (I never earned enough.) Once I was pointed in the direction of physics, I became obsessed by the subject — drunk on it. That feeling is very hard to convey and would make tedious reading if I did try to express it. The experiences I have been describing occurred in and around the edges and interstices of my obsession with physics. But, being rather solitary, I had a great deal of time to think about these experiences, to make them part of some interior mythology. When I began to write this book, I sifted through letters and other memorabilia from those times — I have never kept a diary — and was amazed to discover how this interior mythology had distorted some of the experiences. I found that I had whole years wrong. Writing about these early years, then, was a process of discovery for me.

For that reason I have stopped writing my history at this point. Once I began to write professionally, often about experiences I had had recently, my pieces became a kind of running autobiography. In that sense professional writing meant a loss of innocence — a growing up. Things that now happen to me automatically become grist for the writer's mill in a way that these early experiences never were. They just happened. I have no regrets about this evolution of my life. It has given me much joy. But it is a book that has in many ways already been written.